STAR SAILOR

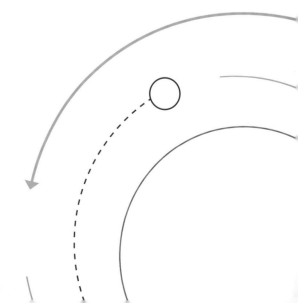

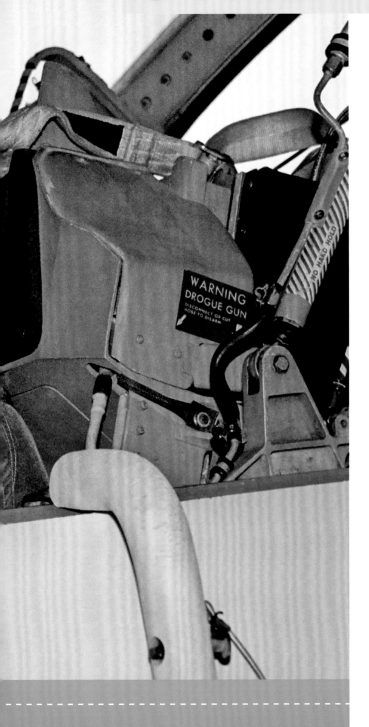

STAR SAILOR

My Life as a NASA Astronaut

Charles F. Bolden Jr.
with Tonya Bolden

CANDLEWICK PRESS

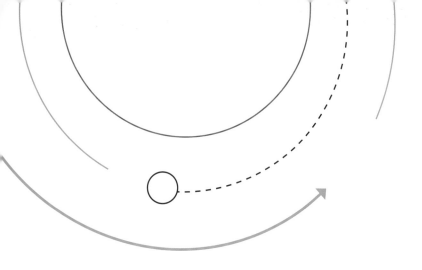

Cover photographs courtesy of NASA
Additional image credits appear on page 98.

First edition 2024

Library of Congress Catalog Card Number pending
ISBN 978-1-5362-1632-5

24 25 26 27 28 29 CCP 10 9 8 7 6 5 4 3 2 1

Printed in Shenzhen, Guangdong, China

This book was typeset in Source Serif Pro.

Candlewick Press
99 Dover Street
Somerville, Massachusetts 02144

www.candlewick.com

A JUNIOR LIBRARY GUILD SELECTION

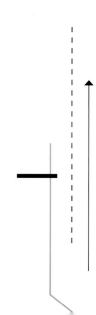

For Mikaley, Kyra, Talia,
Walker, and Lenox
CB

For Kai
TB

Contents

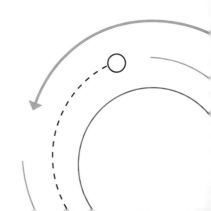

A 2022 "Blue Marble" image of our world. It's based on images taken by Earth Polychromatic Imaging Camera (EPIC) on board the Deep Space Climate Observatory satellite (DSCOVR), on which NASA worked in partnership with the National Oceanic and Atmospheric Administration and the US Air Force.

Delight at Dawn

WE WERE ABOUT FIFTEEN MINUTES into our launch when I glimpsed what I thought was a giant island.

Then I realized that it wasn't an island but our world's second-largest continent, Africa.

Traveling around our planet at a speed of 17,500 miles per hour, we saw a cyclone swirling over the Indian Ocean.

While orbiting Earth every ninety minutes, we lived through *sixteen* sunrises and *sixteen* sunsets every twenty-four hours. Night and day switched back and forth on the surface of Earth every forty-five minutes.

During our six-day mission, I was constantly in awe of the magnificence of our home planet.

That was me, Charlie B., in January 1986, aboard a space shuttle with the same name as the South Carolina city where I was born and raised.

Columbia.

And I was its pilot!

How Fast Is That?

17,500 miles per hour is about five miles per second.

GETTING UP, UP, AND AWAY into space had been a bit of a nightmare.

Delay after delay.

Countdown after countdown.

On the day we were first scheduled to launch, December 18, 1985, the crew never even boarded *Columbia*. We were more than ready—mentally, physically, emotionally—for flight, but the technicians had problems getting all their tools and equipment out of a compartment at the tail end of the shuttle. By the time they did, it was too late to launch.

On the next attempt, after we were all strapped in, there was a weird reading from the hydraulic system of our right-hand solid rocket booster. That time the countdown stopped at T-minus fourteen seconds.

But it turned out to be a false alarm. The technicians later discovered that a bit of debris on a computer card had caused the strange reading. Had we launched, we would've been A-OK—but that's not a chance you take when you're about to ride a rocket.

On another day, the launch was scrubbed because a main engine valve wouldn't close. Had we launched that time, things would *not* have been A-OK. If the valve hadn't closed properly, it could have caused the engine to explode—destroying the vehicle and killing us!

Hydraulic?

Hydraulic comes from the Greek word *hydraulikos,* a combination of the Greek words for water (*hydor*) and pipe (*aulos*). Like the brake system in a car, the shuttle used hydraulic fluid to move different components, such as the landing gear and the three main engines at the tail end of the orbiter. (See pages 10–11 for an orbiter diagram.)

EXTERNAL TANK

SOLID ROCKET BOOSTER

SOLID ROCKET BOOSTER

ORBITER

NASA

Endeavour

Delay after delay, seven in all, including one caused by a fierce thunderstorm.

But then . . .

On January 12, 1986, at NASA's main East Coast launch site, the Kennedy Space Center (KSC) in Cape Canaveral, Florida, at 6:55 a.m. Eastern Standard Time . . .

Liftoff!

A reporter called it "a delight at dawn."

This was *Columbia*'s seventh flight.

But it was my very first time star sailing!

What a ride!

NASA is the acronym for the

NATIONAL

AERONAUTICS AND

SPACE

ADMINISTRATION.

Columbia's liftoff from KSC on January 12, 1986, reflected in the Indian River Lagoon. Believe it or not, I felt quite relaxed and confident—not a twinge of nervousness, nor a hint of anxiety—as all of us on the crew had trained for this day for so long.

NASA's first Black astronauts in 1978, nineteen years after NASA's first class of astronauts. Left to right: Ronald McNair (PhD physicist), Guion "Guy" Bluford Jr. (PhD aerospace engineer, Air Force pilot, and Vietnam veteran), and Frederick Gregory, who earned a bachelor's degree in military engineering and a master's degree in information systems. Like Guy and me, Fred served in Vietnam (helicopter and fighter jet pilot), attended test pilot school, then served as a test pilot.

Thank You, Ron McNair!

I BECAME A STAR SAILOR, or astronaut, in large part thanks to Ron McNair, one of NASA's first Black astronauts.

In the spring of 1979, I was a Marine Corps test pilot at the Naval Air Station at Patuxent River, Maryland, when some NASA astronauts and astronaut candidates who had trained there returned one weekend for a reunion. Physicist Ron McNair, a South Carolinian like me, was one of them.

Before that weekend, I knew that NASA was taking astronaut applications, but applying was the last thing on my mind. In terms of credentials, I had the right stuff. I was a graduate of the US Naval Academy, with a bachelor's degree in electrical science. During the height of the Vietnam War in the early 1970s, I had flown an A-6 Intruder as a Marine Corps pilot on more than a hundred missions in the war zone. What's more, I also had a master's degree in a STEM field: systems management from the University of Southern California.

But . . .

The word *astronaut* comes from two Greek words:
ástron, meaning "star," and *nautes*, meaning "sailor."
But astronauts don't actually get close to the stars!

I felt, well, so ordinary. And even though NASA had three Black astronauts at the time, I had it in my head that astronauts had to be white. Also really, really tall. I was five-seven.

I had forgotten one of my father's favorite sayings: "It's not the size of the dog in the fight, but the size of the fight in the dog." This was Daddy's prime motivator for all of us who played on the high school football team he coached. Our teams won numerous state championships against teams with players much larger than ours.

But all those years later, I simply didn't have the "fight." I lacked the confidence to apply to be an astronaut candidate.

The right credentials. But not the guts.

Then, in that spring weekend of 1979, came Ron. After we met, we spent much of the weekend getting to know each other. While we were hanging out, he asked if I was going to apply.

"Not on your life," I replied.

Ron gave me an odd look. "Why not?"

"Because they'd never pick me."

Ron then eyeballed me *very* strangely. "You know, that's the dumbest thing I've ever heard. How do you know they aren't going to pick you if you never apply?"

I was embarrassed. There was something else I'd forgotten, something my mom and dad had told my younger brother, Warren, and me over and over again: that we could do anything we wanted if we were willing to study and work hard. Our parents also taught us to never let being Black keep us from doing anything we wanted. They constantly told us, "Don't be afraid of failure, and don't let people tell you what you can or cannot do!"

By the time Ron McNair left the Naval Air Station at Patuxent River, I had found the guts. I took out a pen and paper and prepared my application for consideration to be a Marine Corps nominee to become a NASA astronaut (back then, military applicants were first selected by their respective organizations). To my surprise, a few months later, I was selected to be one of fifty

Marine Corps nominees. Within another few months, NASA selected me as one of two hundred finalists chosen for interviews.

In February 1980, I traveled to the Johnson Space Center (JSC) in Houston, Texas, for those interviews and a series of medical and psychological exams. And then I waited.

My wait ended in late May. I got the telephone call informing me that I'd made it in as an astronaut candidate! I was among nineteen applicants NASA accepted that year: eight as shuttle pilot candidates (including me), eleven as candidates to be mission specialists.

On July 1, 1980, my wife, Jackie, our kids, Ché and Kelly, and I headed to JSC, where I began my training. At the time, it was a one-year program.

Our training included classes in astronomy, aerodynamics, meteorology, geography, and geology—plus a three-day field trip to the Grand Canyon to study geological formations of our own home planet, Earth.

There was also bailout training, scuba training, and zero-gravity training (how to deal with weightlessness).

Six months in, we got our technical assignments. That meant working with seasoned astronauts to gain hands-on experience that would prepare us for future space flights.

My first assignment was to work on a "tiger team" with Anna Fisher and Sally Ride, two of NASA's first female astronauts. A tiger team is a group of people with different expertise tasked with solving a problem. Our Fisher-Ride team focused on the shuttle's thermal protection system: the tiles and other materials covering the shuttle to protect it from the extreme heat of reentry on return to Earth. We worked intently to find a process for repairing damaged tile in space.

In the Running

In 1979, **585 people** applied to be shuttle pilot candidates.

A lot more—**2,880**—applied to be mission specialists.

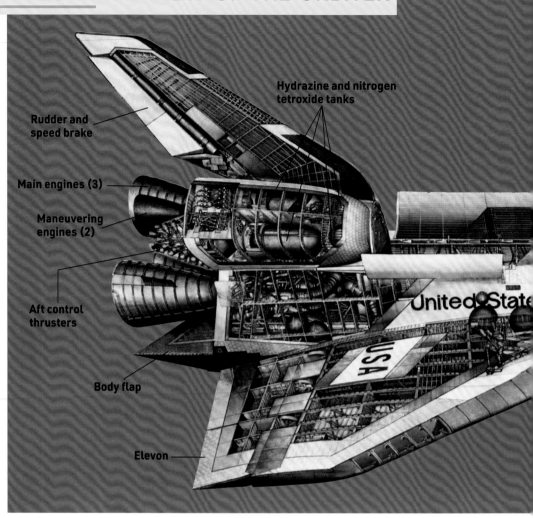

Rudder and speed brake

Main engines (3)

Maneuvering engines (2)

Aft control thrusters

Body flap

Elevon

Hydrazine and nitrogen tetroxide tanks

My training also included becoming a subject matter expert, an authority on one of the shuttle's major systems.

Every major system had an astronaut assigned to it. I was given the auxiliary power units (three in the orbiter and two in each solid rocket booster). The auxiliary power units were essentially pumps that pushed hydraulic fluid to move or activate components in the shuttle system such as the landing gear and brakes and the control surfaces on the wings and tail that allowed pilots to steer the orbiter.

I was also the subject matter expert on the automatic landing system, or

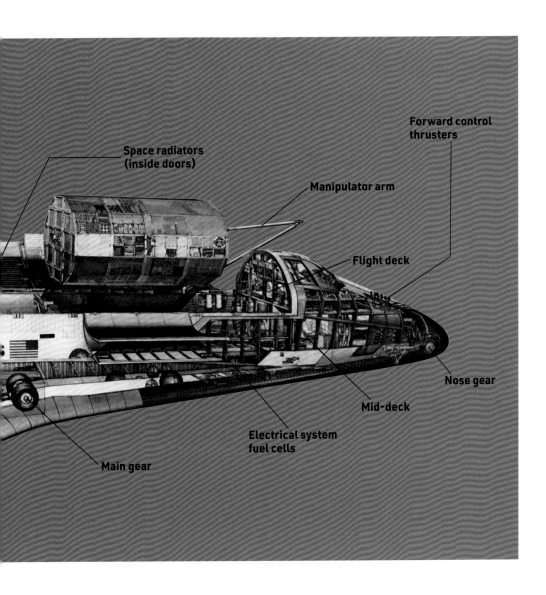

Space radiators
(inside doors)

Manipulator arm

Forward control
thrusters

Flight deck

Nose gear

Mid-deck

Electrical system
fuel cells

Main gear

autoland, which was what it sounds like: a system that allowed onboard computers to fly the orbiter all the way to touchdown.

My months of training were exciting—working with so many talented people, learning so much, taking on challenge after challenge. And my role model Ron McNair was there for me every step of the way as a mentor and friend. Ron took me under his wing and sponsored me when I pledged for Omega Psi Phi, a historic Black fraternity (one of the Divine Nine). Both he and my father had been members since their college days.

Early on in my training, I had a big disappointment: no time in the Shuttle

Mission Simulator (SMS)—a training device built to look and feel exactly like the real shuttle cockpit. At the outset, I didn't realize that only astronauts assigned to an upcoming flight could use the SMS. But then, because of my work on autoland, I caught a break.

My classmate John Blaha was working on a new heads-up display (HUD) that would allow pilots to see all the landing data projected just in front of the shuttle's forward windows. With the HUD, pilots wouldn't have to look back into the cockpit display panels for this information.

John and I convinced the engineers and the training team that we needed to have an opportunity to fly the "real" shuttle simulator. Why? So that we would know how flying the shuttle would look and feel before traveling out to NASA's Ames Research Center in California to fly the Vertical Motion Simulator (VMS), which flew and landed much like the shuttle but didn't have the realistic look in the cockpit of the SMS.

John and I were allowed one two-hour training session in the SMS to prepare for conducting all our engineering tests for the heads-up display and autoland in the VMS.

The SMS was set up so that it was as if we began flying at ten thousand feet, aligned straight into the runway. This allowed us to fly the very last portion of the landing using the heads-up display for our information. We alternated between landing with autoland and manual control to gather data that would allow us to compare the two methods of control all the way to touchdown.

That was unbelievably thrilling. John and I wanted to do more!

We asked the training team to program the simulator with the shuttle up in space so that we could fly a complete reentry into Earth's atmosphere all the way to the ground. We were about fifteen minutes into the half-hour reentry when the simulator suddenly stopped.

The chief of the Astronaut Office had a speaker box in his office that enabled him to monitor every SMS session. He had detected that John and I were doing more than we'd been authorized to do, and so it was game over for us!

NASA Centers and Support Facilities

Plum Brook Station
Sandusky, OH

Lewis Research Center
Cleveland, OH

IV&V Facility
Fairmont, WV

Goddard Space Flight Center
Greenbelt, MD

**Goddard Institute
for Space Studies**
New York, NY

Wallops Flight Facility
Wallops Island, VA

NASA Headquarters
Washington, DC

Langley Research Center
Hampton, VA

**Ames Research
Center**
Moffett Field, CA

**Dryden Flight
Research Center**
Edwards, CA

**Jet Propulsion
Laboratory**
Pasadena, CA

**White Sands
Test Facility**
Las Cruces, NM

**Johnson Space
Center**
Houston, TX

**Michoud
Assembly Facility**
New Orleans, LA

**Marshall Space
Flight Center**
Huntsville, AL

Stennis Space Center
Stennis Space Center, MS

Kennedy Space Center
Kennedy Space Center, FL

This map shows the NASA centers and support facilities that existed when I was an astronaut candidate, along with the Jet Propulsion Laboratory, which is not a NASA center, as frequently thought, but a federally funded research facility known around the world for its development of missions to study planets in our solar system. Like the other candidates training at JSC—the "Home of the Astronauts"—I visited all the NASA centers and facilities in my year of candidacy. These visits allowed us to see all the diverse work of the agency. The Marshall Space Flight Center, for example, is considered the home of large rocket engine development, and Langley Research Center is the oldest NASA center and specializes in research and development of aircraft and the systems to operate them. (Several of these locations have since been renamed. The Dryden Flight Research Center became the Armstrong Flight Research Center, the Lewis Research Center became the Glenn Research Center, Plum Brook Station became the Neil Armstrong Test Facility, and the IV&V Facility became the Katherine Johnson Independent Verification and Validation [IV&V] Facility.)

That chief was retired Navy captain John Young, a legendary Apollo moon walker and commander of the first space shuttle mission in April 1981, a mission aboard *Columbia*.

Four months later, I got the glorious news that I had made the grade to be a space shuttle pilot! Charlie B. was an astronaut!

Autoland in Action?

The Space Shuttle program never used autoland for an actual shuttle landing. The theory that it would be more reliable and accurate than manual landings wasn't supported by the data we collected over months of testing in the VMS.

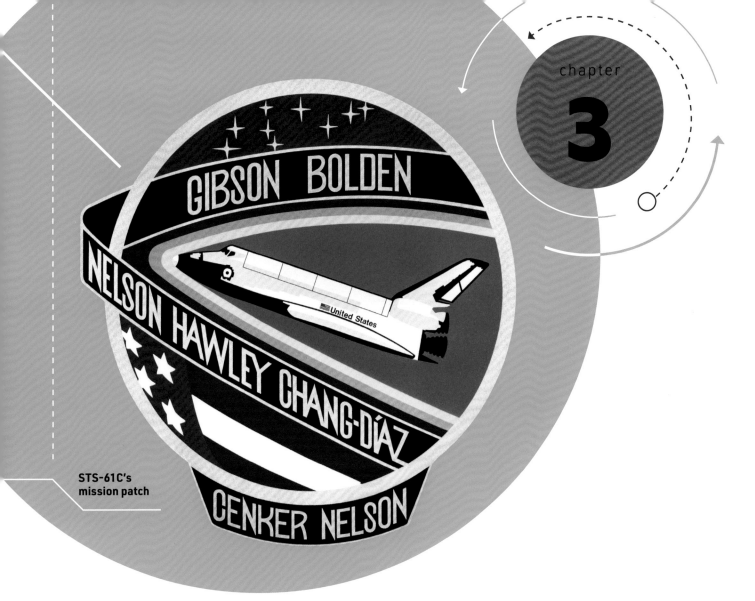

STS-61C's mission patch

Tick, Tick, Tick

TECHNICALLY, a space shuttle mission was a Space Transportation System (STS) mission. When I made my first journey into space aboard *Columbia*, I was part of mission STS-61C. Its primary objective was to deploy a communications satellite that would beam down radio and television signals while orbiting Earth.

In the foreground, left to right: Steve Hawley, Franklin Chang-Díaz, and Robert "Hoot" Gibson. In the background, left to right: Bob Cenker, Bill Nelson, George "Pinky" Nelson, and me. The two Nelsons weren't related. The latter was nicknamed Pinky shortly after he was born because of his complexion at the time. Hoot? Long ago there was a famous cowboy actor named Hoot Gibson. As Commander Gibson explained, for boys of his generation, "If your last name is Gibson, you're most likely going to get 'Hoot' for a nickname."

Who Did What Aboard a Space Shuttle?

Mission specialists, astronauts with a science or an engineering background, had an array of duties, from overseeing experiments and research, to monitoring fuel, food, and drinks, to performing spacewalks if a mission called for one.

Payload specialists were originally experts on a specific payload (cargo). They were picked by NASA, a research organization, or a business partner of NASA's. Congressman Bill Nelson was a member of the STS-61C crew as a result of an agreement between the NASA Administrator (its head) and congressional leadership. A senator and a representative would fly on different shuttle missions. Senator Jake Garn of Utah went first; he flew on *Discovery* in 1985. (In 2021, Bill Nelson became the NASA Administrator.)

Pilots focused on the orbiter systems and, of course, flying and landing the vehicle.

I had six crewmates on this mission. There were three mission specialists: physicist, astronomer, and astrophysicist Steve Hawley; physicist and astronomer Pinky Nelson; and physicist and mechanical engineer Franklin Chang-Díaz, NASA's first Hispanic astronaut. The payload specialists were aerospace and electrical engineer Bob Cenker of RCA and then–US representative Bill Nelson of Florida. Our mission commander, or skipper, was Hoot Gibson, a Vietnam War combat-tested Navy fighter pilot, test pilot, and aeronautical engineer.

"Never, ever wing it!" That's what Hoot preached from day one of our training. We were always to do things by the book, always by established procedure. "No matter how bad things are, you can always make them worse." That was "Hoot's Law"—something that has stayed with me to this day.

There was never a time during my year of candidacy or leading up to my first flight assignment that I doubted my ability to get through the training and fly. But I did have a difficult stretch about six months before my first flight when I got overwhelmed by the amount of information I needed to learn to serve as pilot on the mission. I went to Hoot to talk about it and he offered nothing but encouragement; he told me to hang in there and keep working at it and it would all come out well. He was exactly right—within the next few weeks, everything fell into place.

Several weeks before launch, the crew had the chance to submit personal items and mementos of organizations dear to them, stowed aboard in orbiter lockers. One of the things I decided to bring was a pearl cross belonging to my mom, which I wore while in space.

By our original launch date, the crew had spent *a lot* of time in different simulators, at one point for two to four hours every day. Hoot and I had also spent hours practicing approaches and landings in a Shuttle Training Aircraft, a heavily modified Grumman Gulfstream G-II business jet.

By launch date, the crew had bonded. We were a team. And we were ready! Then came all those delays, until finally—

I'm with (left to right) Pinky, Steve, Bob, and Bill in zero-gravity training. The person in the orange flight suit is a technician, there to help with one of the experiments being evaluated on the flight. We were in a NASA KC-135 (an Air Force transport plane used for aerial refueling and cargo transport) or "Vomit Comet," as it was affectionately called. We usually flew it once in the early part of our training, but might've made additional flights to get an idea of how it would feel to perform an experiment in space where gravity was overcome.

A typical 0-g flight would last about two hours, during which we would do nearly a hundred roller coaster-like maneuvers called "parabolas." The alternate pull-ups and push-overs of the parabolas caused us to go from 2-g to 0-g for about twenty to thirty seconds, causing many on the flight to eventually get sick—thus the name Vomit Comet.

When a rocket lifts off and you're riding it, you don't think of anything but the rocket. I tried to watch all my instruments as I had been trained, but everything was shaking, shaking, shaking—like nothing I'd experienced in any simulation. It was difficult to read anything with any precision.

As we lifted off, I could feel myself sink back into my seat ever so slightly as *Columbia* leaped from KSC's Launch Pad 39A, exerting about 1.5-g on our bodies—about one and a half times the normal force of gravity.

And all was not smooth sailing.

We had just cleared the launch tower when an alarm sounded in the cockpit. With all that shaking still going on, I checked my gauges and warning lights. Everything pointed to a helium leak in one of the shuttle's three main engines.

A helium leak is a big deal!

We needed helium, the same gas used to fill balloons for parties, to control the positions of the main engine valves. One of the critical jobs of these valves after we got into space at a desired speed and altitude was to shut down the main engines by closing off fuel flow while the fuel lines were still pressurized. If the fuel had been allowed to completely drain, we would have had an uncontrolled shutdown of the engines and damage that could have blown off the back end of the orbiter. We never would have survived that, since it would have destroyed the vehicle and us with it.

As the seconds ticked by, I worked the procedure for stopping a helium leak.

Tick,

tick,

tick.

What Is G-Force?

G-force is a unit based on Earth's gravity—on Earth, it's 1-g. But if you're riding a rocket that's rapidly speeding up, the g-force will be greater than 1, and if you're hanging out in space, where gravity is less intense, g-force is less than 1.

Then I noticed that the gauge that had originally signaled a helium leak now indicated that we were *making* helium.

That wasn't possible!

I quickly concluded that it was a computer glitch.

Hoot agreed. He reported this to mission control at JSC while I reconfigured the helium system switches back to their normal positions.

All was now smooth sailing.

AT TWO MINUTES INTO OUR FLIGHT, the solid rocket boosters had almost completely burned out. They separated from their attachments to the external tank and were on their way to a parachute-softened touchdown in the Atlantic Ocean.

About six and a half minutes later, our three main engines shut down—and I no longer felt as if I had an actual gorilla or two sitting on my chest, as I had for the thirty to forty-five seconds before the engines quieted.

At last we were safely in space.

Within seconds, the external tank was released and fell away for its reentry—heating up, expanding, then exploding into thousands of pieces that mostly burned up or splashed into the ocean.

And soon . . .

I saw Africa, where my ancestors had been kidnapped and sold into slavery. They endured the voyage across the Atlantic Ocean in the belly of slave ships and were sold at auction in Charleston, South Carolina.

Tears rolled down my cheeks as I gazed at Africa. From my vantage point, I saw no borders between its countries. It was one beautiful mass of Mediterranean coastal lands giving way to the vast Sahara Desert, then the green equatorial region, and finally, in the distance, the southern section of the continent.

What a powerful reminder of how awful it is that we earthlings so often let differences in skin color or hair texture keep us apart instead of recognizing that we're all created by God as the same, all intended to be equal and free, with no borders or boundaries dividing us.

But I couldn't gaze out the windows of *Columbia* for too long.

We had work to do!

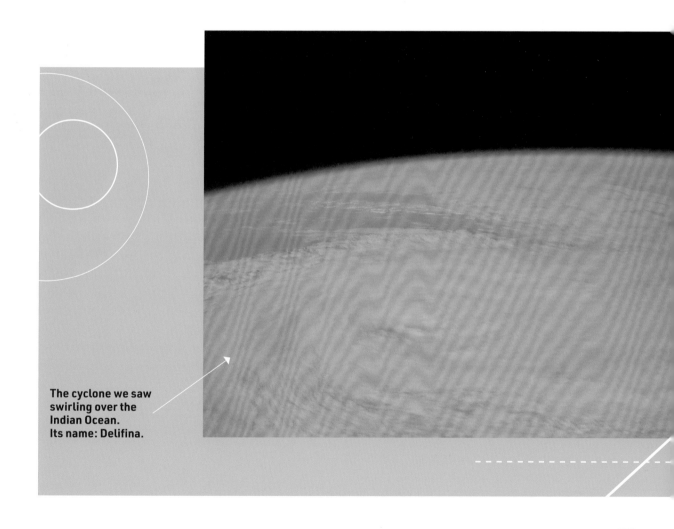

The cyclone we saw swirling over the Indian Ocean. Its name: Delifina.

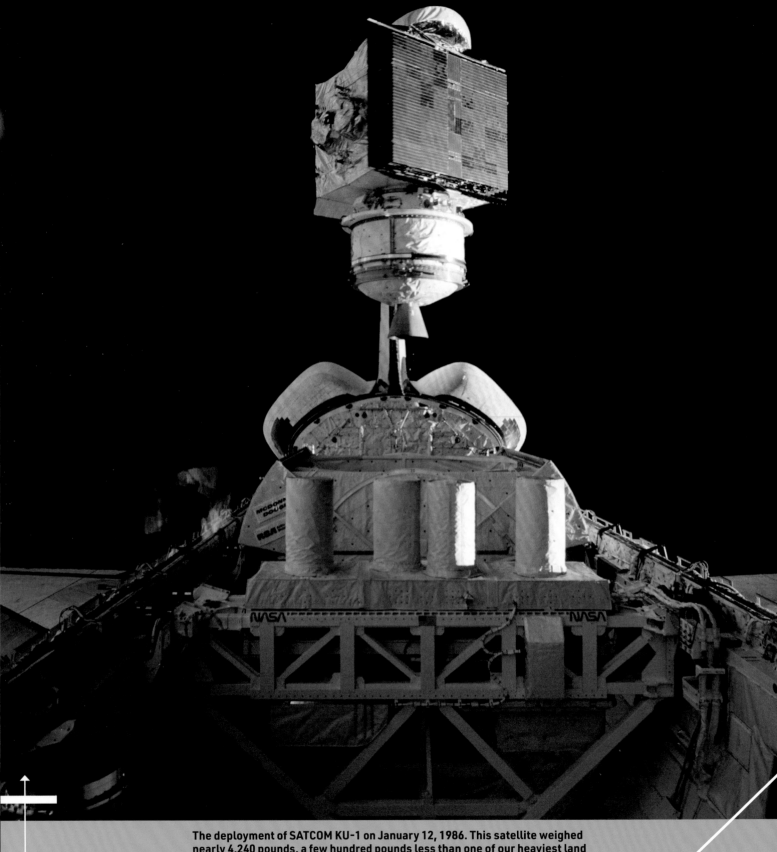

The deployment of SATCOM KU-1 on January 12, 1986. This satellite weighed nearly 4,240 pounds, a few hundred pounds less than one of our heaviest land mammals, the Indian rhino. The satellite's cost of $50 million in the 1980s is equivalent to well over $100 million today.

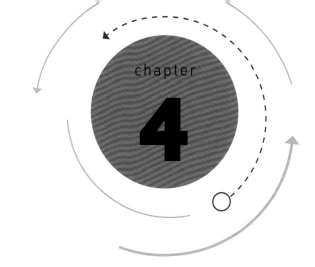
Floating Above My Seat

THE COMMUNICATIONS SATELLITE that we were tasked with deploying was RCA Americom's SATCOM KU-1

Its purpose: to provide US government agencies and private enterprises with voice and data services and KU band video that would bring cable TV into homes and offices across the United States.

Mission accomplished on day one! With Pinky and Franklin handling the deployment and Bob observing, it all went off without a hitch.

With the orbiter perfectly still, SATCOM KU-1 rose up from its payload bay mounting table—spinning, spinning, spinning up to a speed that would keep it stable. (Imagine a spinning top rotating so fast that it stabilizes and looks as though it's standing still.)

Once the satellite attach mechanism was released, a set of springs on the mounting table pushed it away from the shuttle and out into space. Then, when SATCOM KU-1 was

KU?

The KU band is a range of radio waves, including the ones we often use to transmit television, radio, and other communications.

a safe distance from the shuttle, its solid fuel booster engine fired up, and off the satellite went to its operational orbit: the circle around Earth from where it would beam its TV signals back to our planet.

ON DEPLOY DAY and through the days that followed, the crew worked on an assortment of experiments.

One had to do with cancer research.

Another with the impact of microgravity (weightlessness) on human bodies (muscle atrophy and bone loss, for example).

Yet another experiment sought to come up with a better way to control the foliage-eating, crop-destroying spongy moth and the disease-spreading American dog tick. (You probably didn't know astronauts play with bugs just like kids do.)

Some of the experiments had been submitted by high school and college students. For example, a study on the effect of microgravity on the hatching of brine shrimp eggs came from Booker T. Washington High School in Houston.

AFTER THE DEPLOYMENT of SATCOM KU-1, the project we were most psyched about was the Comet Halley Active Monitoring Program (CHAMP). Our mission was to carry out wide-ranging observations of Halley's Comet, which was fast approaching the sun. It hadn't passed that close to Earth in more than seventy years.

Sadly, with CHAMP—mission not accomplished!

A special device for a 35 mm camera, a light intensifier, wouldn't work. Battery problem. The device had been accidentally left on during our launch delays.

On top of that, we had zero luck catching even a glimpse of this most famous comet through our binoculars. The bright light of the sun and the moon prevented us from finding the dimmer comet in the dark sky.

The Most Famous "Dirty Snowball"

Halley's Comet was named after English astronomer Edmond Halley. In 1705, he figured out that comets sighted in 1531, 1607, and 1682 weren't three different comets but the same one. Halley's Comet zooms by Earth every seventy-six years or so.

Comets—masses of ice, rock, dust, and frozen gases—are often called "dirty snowballs" or "icy dirt balls."

UNLIKE WITH CHAMP, we had terrific success with Earth observations. No equipment failures there. We took thousands of photographs and ran through reels and reels of film making videos.

The Irrawaddy River Delta in Myanmar . . . wave action around Western Australia's Beagle Islands . . . the Himalayas . . . the Horn of Africa . . . Chile. Such stunning views of Earth were powerful reminders of the importance of taking care of our planet.

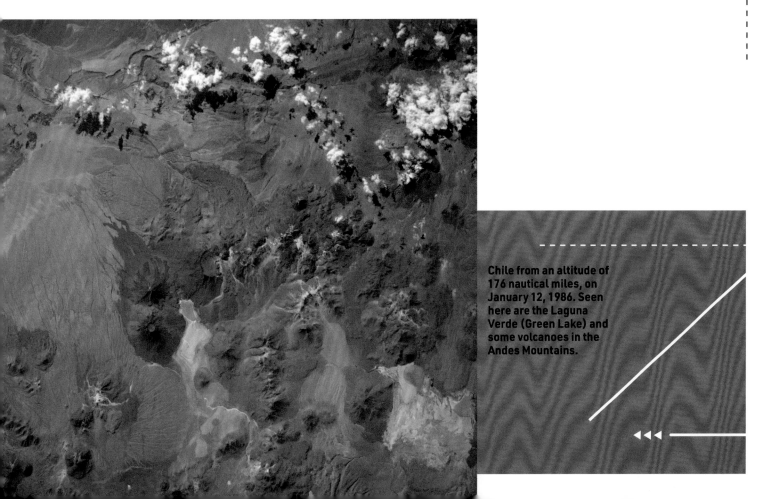

Chile from an altitude of 176 nautical miles, on January 12, 1986. Seen here are the Laguna Verde (Green Lake) and some volcanoes in the Andes Mountains.

BEING IN SPACE wasn't always a thrill a minute. There were chores to do.

Cameras had to be loaded with film. Equipment had to be stowed away. Filters in our air-conditioning system had to be changed twice daily. The shuttle had to be vacuumed. Coffee stains had to be wiped clean where stray droplets had escaped from a drink straw and splattered on a locker surface, the ceiling, or the floor.

When it came to food, we had some fresh fruit for the first couple of days, but after that, everything we ate was precooked and dehydrated, based on the choices we'd made in advance—and there had been plenty of choices.

Prepping our food was a snap.

Add a couple ounces of water to a dehydrated food like scrambled eggs, cereal, oatmeal, grits, green beans, collard greens, corn, or shrimp cocktail, and pop anything we wanted hot into the food warmer along with precooked meats like sausage, ham, or steak. The meats were cooked and packed in foil containers that were radiated to provide long-term stabilization and protection against bacteria and other spoiling agents.

To make milk, coffee, tea, or a fruity drink, grab the right foil package filled with powder and add about eight ounces of hot or cold water.

Eating our meals wasn't always a snap, however.

You had to find somewhere to eat where you wouldn't be in the way of a working crewmate. And you had to find a spot where you could wedge yourself in so you'd remain still long enough to eat.

The only time we normally ate together was for the evening meal. We all floated into the mid-deck and found a favorite place to hover with our meals as we talked about the day or life in general.

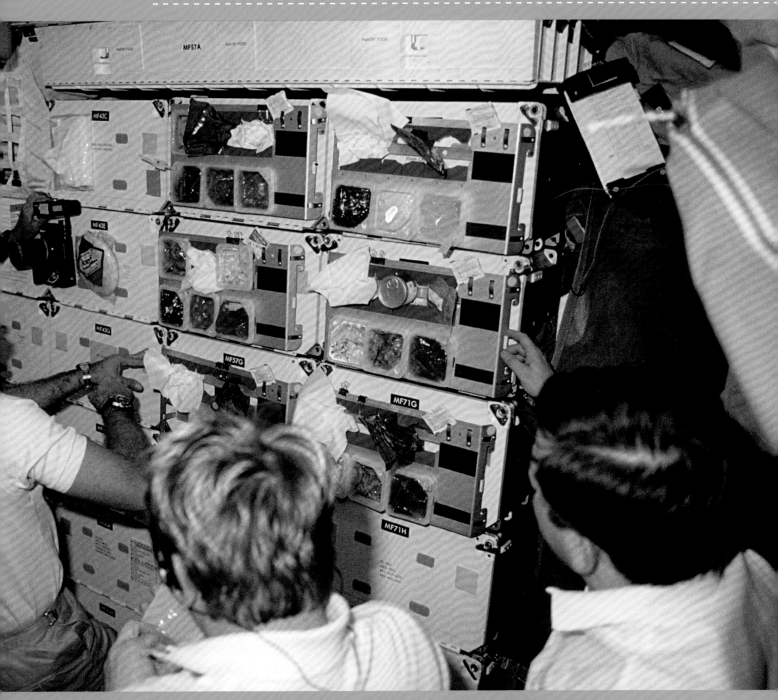

Chow time! I'm with Hoot, Pinky, and Bob in the mid-deck. Containers of food and drink were color coded. (All my selections had yellow dots.) That way, if need be, one person could prepare meals for the rest of the crew. The taste of space food? Great!

When it was time for our eight-hour sleep period, we turned off the interior lights, floated into sleep restraints, and zipped ourselves in. Imagine lightweight sleeping bags with strips of Velcro. With that Velcro, we could attach ourselves to the shuttle's walls, ceiling, floor—almost anywhere—so that we wouldn't float all over the place while asleep. I opted to tie one end of my sleep restraint to the rudder pedal in front of my seat on the flight deck, and so I slept floating above my seat.

I also used Velcro to attach a set of cameras with a variety of lenses by the window for when I woke up so I could photograph parts of Earth that were in darkness during our workday but in daylight while we slept. These were usually areas of specific interest to me that weren't important enough to make it onto the official list of Earth observation photos to be taken.

AS WITH OUR LAUNCH, STS-61C's return to Earth had delays. More than once, bad weather kept us from landing at KSC. Finally, after two days of bad weather in Florida, the mission managers directed Hoot and me to reprogram our computers for a landing in California, at Edwards Air Force Base (AFB) in the Mojave Desert. It would be a night landing, only the second one in what was then NASA's twenty-four space shuttle missions. Because emergency landings and rescues are more challenging in the dark, day landings were always the first choice. But we'd already delayed our landing for a few days, and we didn't want to risk running out of consumables—necessary items like food and oxygen.

Hoot and I were as ready as we could be for our night landing. Hoot, who lived by the rule that we had to be prepared for any- and everything, had decided early on that when it came to landing, half of our training would be for doing so in the dark.

Once we were all set to come home, as we had trained to do hundreds of times, Hoot maneuvered *Columbia* into the proper attitude (position and orientation) for the "deorbit burn" (rocket engine firing). That slowed us down by

Me, Charlie B., in the pilot's station in the flight deck before reentry into Earth's atmosphere. I tried to strike a balance between being excited and overly relaxed about this phase of the journey.

The Friction Factor

If you rub your hands together repeatedly really fast, you'll feel the heat created by the friction of your hands pushing against each other. It's the same thing that happened when *Columbia* entered Earth's atmosphere and molecules of air rushed past the bottom of the orbiter, creating more and more heat as the density of the air increased.

about three hundred miles per hour—just enough to allow gravity to overcome the forces that had been keeping the shuttle in its circular orbit of Earth.

Gently, *Columbia* fell back toward Earth. In thirty minutes, we reached Earth's atmosphere, about four hundred thousand feet above the surface.

Columbia then started to enter Earth's atmosphere at an altitude and geographic position called "entry interface."

As the atmosphere became denser by the minute, the tiles on the bottom of the shuttle heated up more and more, as we knew they would.

From inside the crew cabin, we could see the glow through the windows from the protective tiles on the bottom of the orbiter. As the temperature increased, reaching over 3,000 degrees Fahrenheit, the light from the hot tiles prevented us from seeing anything else out the window. As we got deeper into the atmosphere, the heating receded and the glow eventually disappeared, allowing us to see outside again.

The lights of the western United States were soon in view. We were well out over the Pacific Ocean, about a thousand miles from our landing site.

Finally, after an almost hour-long reentry, a gliding *Columbia* slowed to just under the speed of sound. We felt a sudden but mild (and totally expected) vibration as the vehicle made its transition from supersonic to subsonic flight.

How Hot Is That?

When heated to 3,090 degrees Fahrenheit, sand melts into glass. The orbiter's tiles didn't melt because they were made of a material called silica that is essentially a type of very high-temperature blown sand that would require temperatures well over 3,000 degrees Fahrenheit to melt.

On the ground, at Edwards AFB and all along the West Coast, folks had heard the double sonic *BOOM-BOOM*!

Columbia was ready to land.

When our spaceplane was about seven miles above Earth, I took the controls and began to fly it on its descending, circular approach to the landing runway. About halfway around, Hoot took the controls and followed the navigation instruments, the variety of landing aids in the cockpit, and the lights on the ground. He soon brought *Columbia* to a perfect, pinpoint touchdown on Edwards AFB's floodlit three-mile-long runway 22.

It was Saturday, January 18, 5:58:51 a.m. Pacific Standard Time, seventy-two minutes before the break of dawn.

Gently, Hoot applied the brakes. In just under a minute, *Columbia* came to a stop.

Total mission time: six days, two hours, three minutes, and fifty-one seconds.

We had traveled 2.5 million miles.

The Speed of Sound

The speed of sound at sea level is about 761 miles per hour, or about 1,100 feet per second. *Supersonic* means traveling faster than the speed of sound; *subsonic* means traveling slower than the speed of sound.

TOUCHDOWN! ↓

ON THE DAY we'd launched, Fred Gregory, NASA's first Black shuttle pilot, called out over the radio to me, "Welcome to space, rookie."

Six days later, I was a rookie no more! Charlie B., NASA's fourth Black astronaut to journey into space and its second Black pilot, was now a real, genuine, no-doubt-about-it, experienced astronaut!

AFTER PHYSICAL EXAMS and other tests at Edwards AFB, the crew was flown to Houston's Ellington Field, a few miles from JSC.

When we stepped off the plane, family members were at the base of the aircraft steps. Soon, we were all on our way to the NASA flight line for the official welcome home ceremony.

THE CREW HAD THE NEXT DAY OFF—sort of. We had to go through all the photos and video we had taken to put together a slide and film presentation that told the story of our mission. We showed this presentation during a crew press conference a few days later.

For about a week after landing, we had debriefs. In these meetings with flight controllers, trainers, medical personnel, and members of management, we recounted every detail of every aspect of the mission, from preflight training to post-landing medical exams.

The day of our last debrief, we huddled in JSC's Astronaut Office conference room with many other astronauts to watch, via closed-circuit TV, mission commander Dick Scobee and six fellow astronauts lift off

We were beyond happy to see our families at Ellington Field. It felt so good to hug my wife, Jackie, our daughter, Kelly, and our son, Ché. We were supposed to land at KSC, so that's where our families had been waiting. After the decision was made to have us land at Edwards AFB, NASA arranged for our families to be flown to Ellington. They arrived about half an hour before we did.

from KSC's Launch Pad 39B in space shuttle *Challenger*. This was mission STS-51L, the first teacher-in-space mission. Christa McAuliffe was that teacher, and Ron McNair, my role model, mentor, and friend, was a mission specialist.

IT WAS FREEZING COLD at the launch site that morning. The launchpad crew had significant difficulty closing and locking the shuttle's crew hatch. Then came whipping winds. After an extensive delay, the launch was scrubbed for the day.

The next morning, Tuesday, January 28, our crew was back in the Astronaut Office conference room to watch *Challenger* launch.

It was freezing cold that day, too. But this time there was no problem with the crew hatch. There wasn't one hiccup. Liftoff was at approximately 11:37 a.m.

But then, seventy-three seconds into flight—an apparent explosion.

At first I thought maybe the solid rocket boosters had separated from the shuttle too early, that *Challenger* would simply have to abort (fly back to the shuttle runway at KSC to land).

I held my breath, watching, hoping, praying that we'd see *Challenger* fly out of the plume of smoke and fire.

But no. The brave crew and space shuttle *Challenger* were gone.

It was NASA's first loss of a space shuttle and its crew.

IN THE HOURS, days, and weeks to come, like all my fellow astronauts, I went through swings of emotions.

I wondered about the future of the Space Shuttle program.

I wondered about my future with NASA.

But it wasn't long before I decided that I owed it to Ron and to the rest of *Challenger*'s crew to stay with NASA, to work to find out what had gone wrong, and to get it fixed so that the USA could get back to human space exploration, to conducting potentially life-changing research in space, and to carrying out observations of our awesome planet, Earth.

The *Challenger* crew. Front row, left to right: pilot Michael Smith, mission commander Francis "Dick" Scobee, and my dear friend Ron McNair. Back row, left to right: mission specialist Ellison Onizuka, payload specialist Christa McAuliffe, payload specialist Gregory Jarvis, and mission specialist Judith Resnik. After the tragedy, for the next year or so, the Bolden family became a second family for Ron's widow, Cheryl, and their two children, Reggie and Joy. Reggie was almost four years old and Joy was eighteen months old when they lost their dad.

Risky Business

IN THE WAKE of the *Challenger* disaster, I was made the new head of NASA's Johnson Space Center Safety Division. This essentially put me in charge of NASA's efforts to revamp its safety program for future human spaceflights. I was granted authority to increase the size of the Safety Division, to hire people with engineering expertise and skills the division lacked at the time of the accident.

Among my new hires was a physics professor at Prairie View A&M University named Ervin Emanuel. He was a registered professional electrical engineer and an expert in electrical power systems. He helped us evaluate the causes of the accident and potential solutions so we could reduce the risk of another catastrophe.

What happened to *Challenger* stemmed from a failure in its right-hand solid rocket booster that allowed hot gases to escape through one of the joints connecting two of the lower segments of that booster. The escaping gas was so hot that it melted the lower attach fitting that held the solid rocket booster in place on the side of the external tank. Once the tail end of the booster broke free, the top rotated into the side of the external tank and punctured its liquid oxygen tank. This caused the external tank to explode. That, in turn, caused the crew module to break away from the rest of the orbiter and fall into the Atlantic Ocean, where it broke up upon impact.

While we in the Safety Division did our utmost to keep another deadly accident from happening, we knew that no matter how hard we worked and how many changes we made, human spaceflight would always be a risky business.

IT WAS A LONG, difficult road to recovery, but NASA did it! Nearly three years after *Challenger*, on the morning of Thursday, September 29, 1988, commander Rick Hauck and four other experienced star sailors, including my former crewmate Pinky Nelson, launched from KSC aboard space shuttle *Discovery* on mission STS-26.

They returned safely to Earth four days later.

During their mission, the crew deployed a satellite and conducted lots of experiments. They also tested out a slew of changes that had been made to the orbiter after the *Challenger* disaster.

With STS-26's success, the Space Shuttle program was back in business.

Eighteen months later, I was piloting *Discovery*.

Our main mission: to deploy a mighty big eye in the sky that could explore our universe from space in a way that was never before possible.

That eye in the sky was the $1.5 billion, roughly 24,000-pound, 43.5-foot-long Hubble Space Telescope, named after American astronomer Edwin Hubble, who in the 1920s discovered that the universe was much vaster than anyone imagined and that there were galaxies beyond our Milky Way.

This observatory, a joint NASA/European Space Agency project, was far more complex and powerful than previous space telescopes, and it was capable of peering deeper into the universe and taking sharper photographs of the cosmos. It was expected to do so for fifteen years.

Boy, was I ecstatic to be a part of mission STS-31, tasked with deploying this magnificent instrument—and with a terrific team at that.

STS-31's mission commander was US Air Force test pilot and aeronautical engineer Loren Shriver. The mission specialists were my former crewmate Steve Hawley; retired Navy captain, pilot, and electrical engineer Bruce McCandless; and geologist and

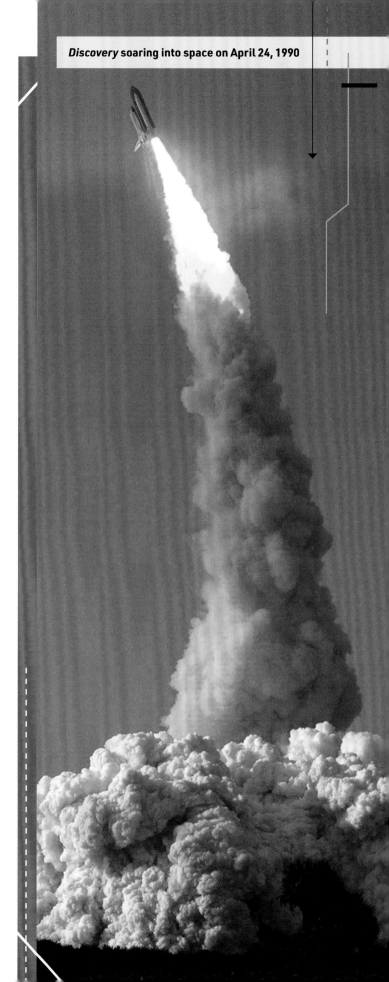

Discovery soaring into space on April 24, 1990

oceanographer Kathy Sullivan, the first American woman to walk in space (1984). Kathy and Bruce were absolute experts on Hubble. They had been involved with its development for several years and knew it up and down, inside and out.

OUR PREFLIGHT TRAINING as an entire crew began at JSC in late 1988.

Like my previous training, it included stand-alone crew training on generic shuttle procedures and integrated crew training with the entire flight control team at JSC, as well as with the teams at the Goddard and Marshall Space Flight centers we'd work with when deploying Hubble.

Loren and I spent hours in the Shuttle Training Aircraft, and there was T-38 jet training for the entire crew. At JSC and at Marshall, Bruce and Kathy had spacewalk training.

No one had to tell us about the need to maintain a healthy lifestyle, from diet to exercise. We all knew that a healthy lifestyle was just as important to remaining an astronaut as it was to becoming one.

The choice of physical training was left up to each crew member. At JSC, we had a full complement of workout gear in the Astronaut Gym, along with racquetball, squash, and handball courts. We also had a strong intramural sports program, and many of the offices at JSC sponsored their own competitive teams. (I played on the Astronaut Office basketball, soccer, and softball teams. I wasn't great in any of those sports. I played for the fun and camaraderie.)

IN READYING OURSELVES for STS-31, we spent a lot of time in simulators, doing stand-alone training with only our crew and our training team—getting to know the orbiter all over again, refreshing our skills. That was during the first six months.

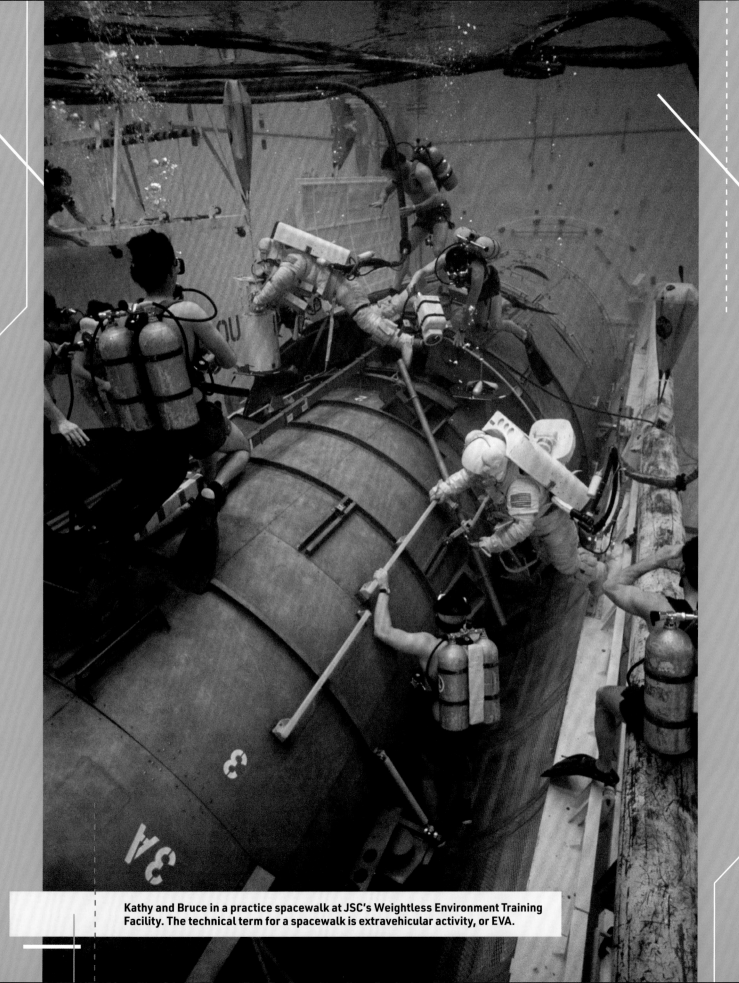

Kathy and Bruce in a practice spacewalk at JSC's Weightless Environment Training Facility. The technical term for a spacewalk is extravehicular activity, or EVA.

Then came the hard part: six-plus months of simulator training, with the flight control team calling the shots from mission control. This training was focused on getting the flight control team ready and allowing us to rely more heavily on them to monitor and manage the orbiter systems in flight. They had much more detailed insight into the health of all the systems than we had onboard—in both the SMS and the actual orbiter.

The training team's job was to get us into trouble—that is, to come up with case after case of something going wrong, something we had to detect, then correct. Though at times the training team made us miserable, we were grateful for their work. They were exposing us to every conceivable failure and providing us with confidence that we could handle any situation, both in training and in flight.

OUR LAST worst-case training scenario before our launch had to do with a solar array, one of Hubble's two twenty-five-foot-long winglike solar panels that would provide it with electrical power from sunlight. The solar arrays would also send excess power to Hubble's batteries. This stored-up power would keep Hubble functioning during the thirty-six minutes of its approximately ninety-seven-minute orbit when it wouldn't be in sunlight but in Earth's shadow.

What if a solar array failed to open on deploy day?

That was the problem we were given, one that mission control couldn't solve. In that case, Kathy and Bruce would do a spacewalk and manually open the solar array.

I was the support crew member for the spacewalk (the intervehicular crewmate, or the IV person). It would be my job to go with Kathy and Bruce down to the mid-deck to help them into their spacesuits, then see them into the airlock and start depressurizing it. Once they were out in space, I would talk them through the process of using a special wrench to roll out the solar array.

A solar array at British Aerospace in Bristol, England

Technicians engaged in testing Hubble's body at the Lockheed Martin assembly plant

The entire crew learned how to open a solar array manually. That training took place in Bristol, England, at British Aerospace, where the solar arrays were built.

Hubble's body, about the size and weight of the average school bus, was built at a Lockheed Martin plant in Sunnyvale, California. The crew visited that plant, as well as other production plants, several times before our launch. Those Sunnyvale visits included training on Hubble.

Steve and I practiced activating controls for things such as electrical power, umbilical release, and other operations we'd perform on orbit. Bruce and Kathy were able to touch real components so they would understand how the observatory was constructed and what the actual components looked like.

We also spent time with people who were working on Hubble, thanking them for their efforts. And we had a lot of fun during school visits and other outreach activities near the plants we visited.

SPACE SHUTTLE *DISCOVERY* launched from KSC at 8:33:51 a.m. Eastern Daylight Time on Tuesday, April 24, 1990. To get Hubble safely deployed in space, we had to fly in a circular orbit of 400 nautical miles—150 miles higher than any shuttle had flown before.

From launch to orbit, everything was flawless.

Not so on the next day, Hubble deploy day.

Problem number one: With Steve operating a fifty-foot remote manipulator system (RMS—a robotic arm) and me serving as backup, we had trouble getting Hubble out of the payload bay. It wasn't Steve's fault. The RMS was moving in ways we hadn't experienced in simulations. It had Hubble twisting, turning, and rolling instead of rising straight up and out of the payload bay.

Steve had to shift to a backup mode of operating the RMS called single joint ops. This meant individually selecting one joint to move at a time in lifting the telescope. It worked fine, but what had taken about fifteen minutes in our training sessions at JSC took more than an hour on deploy day.

Problem number two: Once Hubble was grappled with the RMS and raised out of the payload bay, the first solar array rolled out and locked into place as programmed—but not the second one. It rolled out about sixteen inches and then quit moving. Stuck!

Bruce was certain there was a problem with the tension monitoring module, software intended to keep the solar array from unfurling and tearing or otherwise damaging itself if it came under any undue strain. (The rest of us on the crew were absolutely clueless about that software component!)

For the next few hours, flight controllers in Houston and engineers around the world racked their brains trying to understand what had caused the second solar array to jam.

And Hubble didn't have all the time in the world.

In the shuttle's payload bay, Hubble had been connected to the orbiter's power system. But now that it had been lifted from the payload bay, it was operating on its own battery power and would have to do so until the solar arrays began providing power and recharging the batteries.

As I recall, we had six and a half hours of battery life when we lifted Hubble from the payload bay and unplugged it from the orbiter. If Hubble ran out of power, the heaters that kept the telescope alive and functioning would fail. As its components froze, Hubble would have slowly deteriorated. I didn't know how much power, if any, Hubble was getting from the first solar array.

At one point we feared that we would have to bring Hubble back inside the payload bay and scrub the deployment altogether.

Kathy (standing) and me (kneeling), learning to manually open a solar array

Tick. Tick. Tick.

Mission control gave the go-ahead for Kathy and Bruce to prepare for a spacewalk. It would take time to get them suited up—if the engineers back on Earth couldn't find another solution, Kathy and Bruce needed to be ready.

Gulp.

That gulp wasn't from Kathy or Bruce. Like Kathy, Bruce had done a spacewalk before. Both were really looking forward to another one.

That gulp was from me.

In training for spacewalks, I hadn't given much thought to the fact that I would be the last person to verify that all connections on their spacesuits were properly made and all joints tightly connected, locked, and sealed to maintain the suit pressurization that would keep Kathy and Bruce alive once they moved out into the vacuum of space.

With Kathy and Bruce in the airlock, as I closed and locked the hatch and watched the pressure in the airlock drop toward vacuum (to match space), I got a sudden feeling of terror. I prayed that I had not missed anything.

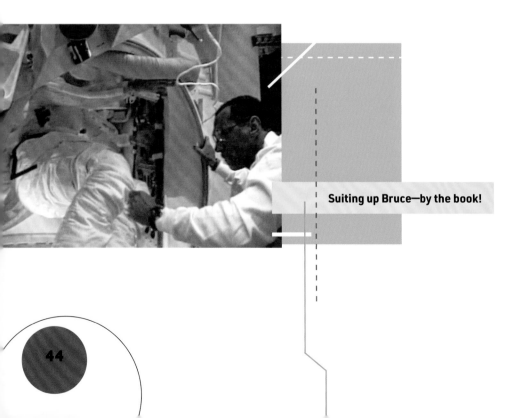

Suiting up Bruce—by the book!

Kathy in the airlock, making final preparations for the spacewalk

chapter

6

What Sound Does a Space Turkey Make?

KATHY AND BRUCE were about five minutes away from opening the airlock hatch and stepping out into space, when—

"Hey, time out. Don't open the hatch yet." That was mission control. "We've got an idea."

Just as Bruce had thought earlier in the day, the folks on the ground suspected that the problem was the tension monitoring module. An engineer at

Goddard had a software fix. He sent a computer command from the ground to "no-op" the module, that is, to ignore any inputs from the module that would stop the movement of the array.

Once that was done, the second solar array unfurled perfectly.

Steve released Hubble from the robotic arm with ease.

That mighty big eye in the sky went into its orbit.

Discovery was above the eastern Pacific Ocean and beginning to fly across South America as Hubble floated away. We had a breathtaking view of this majestic observatory finally flying freely on its own.

Sadly, Kathy and Bruce didn't get to witness this awesome sight. These two people who had devoted so many years of their lives to Hubble were still in the windowless airlock. Not until mission control was certain that everything was truly A-OK did we get the order to repressurize the airlock and let Kathy and Bruce out. They had missed everything!

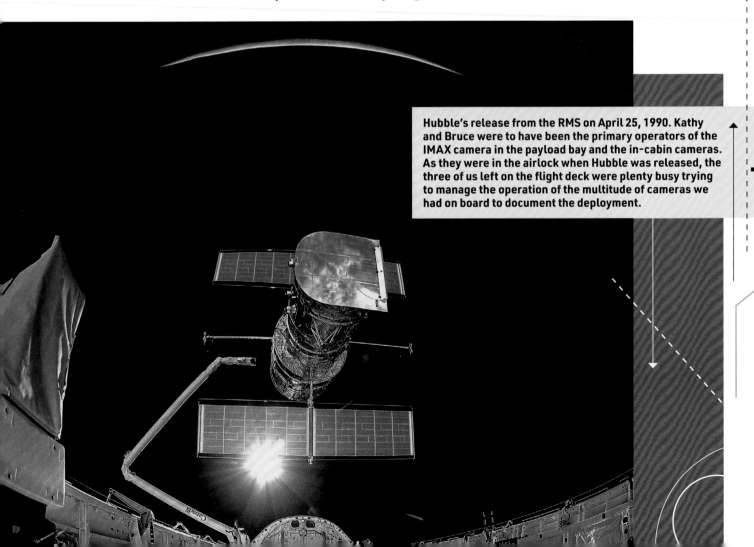

Hubble's release from the RMS on April 25, 1990. Kathy and Bruce were to have been the primary operators of the IMAX camera in the payload bay and the in-cabin cameras. As they were in the airlock when Hubble was released, the three of us left on the flight deck were plenty busy trying to manage the operation of the multitude of cameras we had on board to document the deployment.

It was an exceptionally long and taxing day, emotionally and physically, but we all felt enormously proud of the roles we had played in getting the job done. I think it's fair to say we were also quite humbled by the knowledge that we had been privileged to work with the incredible teams who had trained and prepared us for the mission and with those who had battled through challenge after challenge on deploy day to get Hubble safely to the place in space where it could begin its work in revolutionizing our understanding of the universe.

People had been waiting for that moment for years—decades for some.

"It's hard to go somewhere and find someone who has never heard of the Hubble Space Telescope." That was me a few days after Hubble's deployment, in a press conference from orbit. "It makes little kids light up," I added. "It makes little kids want to learn how to add and subtract and study science."

That press conference was held on the day before our return to Earth. By then we had carried out a host of experiments.

A few days after Hubble's deployment. I can't remember why I chose to float above Kathy. Bruce is holding up a placard of our mission patch. Steve is holding a paper model of Hubble. On the far left is our skipper, Loren.

My favorite was the one submitted by a young man named Greg. It was on the effect of Earth's magnetic field on an electric arc. (Imagine a science-fiction movie with a mad scientist's laboratory containing what looks like a lightning bolt going from one wire to another, or into his monster's head.) Greg had constructed a simple box containing two nail-like metal spikes protruding into the box, which connected to an electric power cable in the mid-deck.

Greg's hypothesis was that in space, the electric arc generated between

Kathy and me monitoring Greg's experiment. Other experiments were aimed at combatting medical conditions, including AIDS and high blood pressure. Fastened to the lockers in the background are some crew mementos. They include a pennant for the Jayhawks, the sports teams of the University of Kansas, where Steve earned his bachelor's degree.

the two spikes when we turned the system's electrical power on would change its shape as we rotated the box and allowed the invisible magnetic field lines of Earth to act on the arc. Amazingly, that's exactly what happened. We saw the arc bow out and flatten as the box's orientation changed. Success for Greg's hypothesis!

I loved Greg's experiment because it was a great example of persistence and determination. He was in high school when he first submitted his experiment and worked for years with a NASA sponsor until his project was finally selected to fly and made it onto STS-31 with us. By that point, he was in medical school.

ON SUNDAY, APRIL 29, 1990, *Discovery* touched down at Edwards AFB, runway 22, at 6:49:57 a.m. Pacific Daylight Time. Mission time: five days, one hour, sixteen minutes, and six seconds.

"Welcome back. Congratulations on a super mission," said spacecraft communicator Steve Oswald from mission control. "The world is waiting to reap the benefits of your work over the next fifteen years."

Discovery on May 7, 1990, returning to the Shuttle Landing Facility at KSC, piggybacked on a Shuttle Carrier Aircraft (a modified Boeing 747)

When we exited *Discovery*, roughly twenty thousand people were there to greet us, and the "The Star-Spangled Banner" was blaring through loud-speakers.

BACK ON SOLID GROUND

Like millions of people around the world, from professional astronomers to schoolkids, the STS-31 crew couldn't wait for Hubble to start beaming down images.

The first one came a few weeks after our return. It was a photograph that included binary star HD96755. But the image was really fuzzy. Hubble had a serious vision problem.

GROUND BASED IMAGE
LAS CAMPANAS OBSERVATORY
CARNEGIE INST. OF WASHINGTON

HUBBLE SPACE TELESCOPE
WIDE FIELD/PLANETARY CAMERA

NASA

On the right is the first image Hubble beamed down, on May 20, 1990. At the top is binary star HD96755. A binary star is two stars so close together that they appear as a single star through most telescopes. On the left is a photograph of the same region of space taken by a ground-based observatory in Chile.

This super-duper telescope was soon the brunt of jokes.

"What sound does a space turkey make?" That was comedian Jay Leno.

Answer: "Hubble, Hubble, Hubble."

Leno also made Hubble a verb: to "Hubble" something meant to really mess it up.

So embarrassing!

But that eventually changed. In December 1993, NASA launched space shuttle *Endeavour* on STS-61 with a seven-member crew to make repairs to Hubble. They installed a large box called COSTAR (Corrective Optics Space Telescope Axial Replacement). COSTAR, about the size of an old-fashioned telephone booth, contained a series of mirrors and lenses to correct a defect in Hubble's primary mirror. They also installed a new set of advanced solar arrays. Soon, that mighty big eye in the sky was beaming down breathtaking images of the cosmos.

Thanks to repairs and upgrades made during four additional servicing missions, the Hubble Space Telescope operated well beyond its planned lifetime of fifteen years. In 2020, Hubble fans celebrated its thirtieth year in orbit.

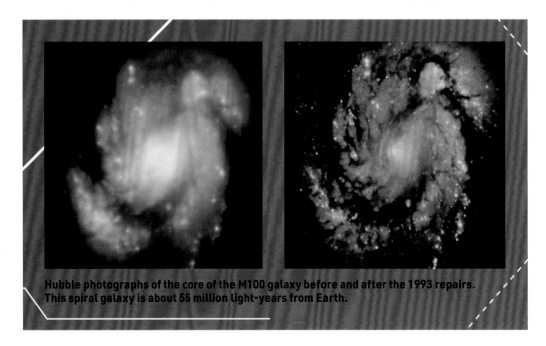

Hubble photographs of the core of the M100 galaxy before and after the 1993 repairs. This spiral galaxy is about 55 million light-years from Earth.

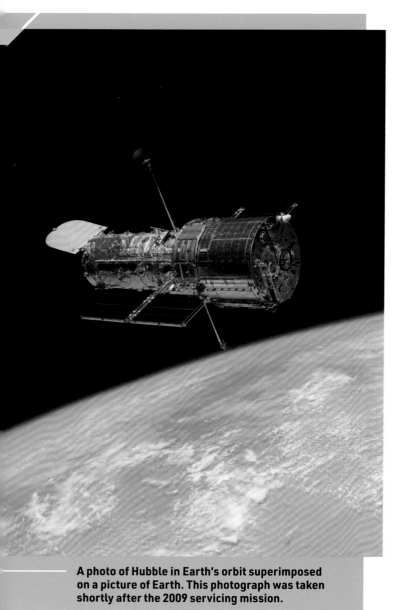

A photo of Hubble in Earth's orbit superimposed on a picture of Earth. This photograph was taken shortly after the 2009 servicing mission.

By the way, my crewmate Bruce played a key role in the development of specialized Hubble tools that were used for each servicing mission.

Hubble fundamentally changed human understanding of the universe and our place in it. Over the years, Hubble confirmed the presence of black holes in the centers of galaxies, for example. It helped scientists determine that the cosmos is 13.8 billion years old. And it discovered that in addition to its large moon, Charon, Pluto has small moons—Nix and Hydra were found in 2005, Kerberos in 2011, and Styx in 2012.

As for me, Charlie B., by the time Hubble was first repaired, I had completed my third mission.

Not as the pilot but as mission commander!

JWST

A year before Hubble was deployed, there was talk of an even mightier eye in the sky, one that was eventually named the James Webb Space Telescope (JWST) after NASA's second Administrator. He headed the agency in the 1960s, during the days of Project Mercury, Project Gemini, and the start of Project Apollo. JWST—developed by NASA, the European Space Agency, and the Canadian Space Agency—was launched on December 25, 2021.

The crew of STS-45 in our launch and entry suits. Seated next to me is pilot Brian Duffy. Standing behind us, left to right: payload specialist Byron Lichtenberg, mission specialists Mike Foale and Dave Leestma, mission specialist and payload commander Kathy Sullivan, and payload specialist Dirk Frimout.

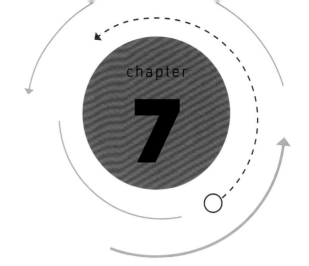
Ignore-o-Sphere

"WE ARE VERY HONORED to assist in recognizing George Lucas, an explorer in his own right."

That was me, Charlie B., in a video beamed down to Earth on March 30, 1992, during the Academy Awards ceremony. George Lucas, creator of the Star Wars series, was receiving a major award for his body of work.

Lucas, I said, "has pushed the boundaries of cinematography and science fiction to excite imaginations and to inspire young and old throughout the world about this new ocean we call space."

Our entire seven-person crew was crowded in the cockpit. In unison, we shouted, "Congratulations, George Lucas, from the crew of *Atlantis*!"

Atlantis starting its roll maneuver just after clearing the launch tower after liftoff. The roll maneuver had two purposes: (1) to orient the vehicle for its flight in the direction of its desired orbit and (2) to verify that the computer commands got through to the vehicle and controlled it as desired.

We were in day six of mission STS-45, part of NASA's Mission to Planet Earth program: an intense study of our home planet, from climate and weather to oceans and forests. This was the first of the Spacelab missions, which began early in the shuttle program to conduct world-class science research in space.

Given the project name Atmospheric Laboratory for Applications and Science (ATLAS), our mission's goal was to study Earth's atmosphere from its lowest layer, the troposphere, to its uppermost layer, the exosphere.

Earth's atmosphere contains a variety of gases that allow us humans to survive—oxygen being especially critical to human life. The more we know about our atmosphere, the better scientists can come up with ways to protect our environment and preserve life on Earth.

STS-45's primary focus was on the third layer, or middle atmosphere: the mesosphere. Scientists nicknamed the mesosphere the "ignore-o-sphere" because it was rarely studied. And atmospheric scientists were convinced that it had a great effect on how weather forms and how the ozone layer behaves, for example.

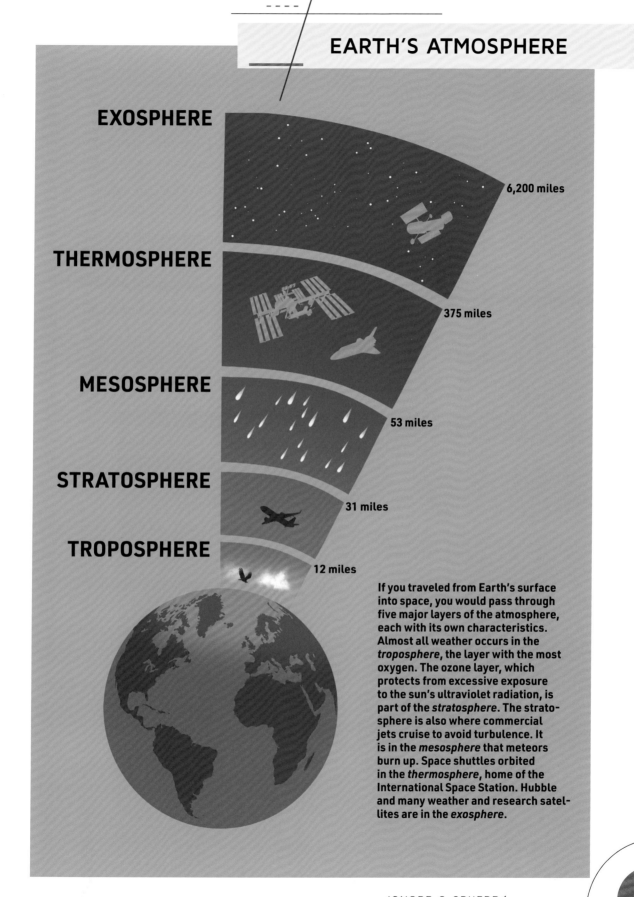

EXOSPHERE

6,200 miles

THERMOSPHERE

375 miles

MESOSPHERE

53 miles

STRATOSPHERE

31 miles

TROPOSPHERE

12 miles

If you traveled from Earth's surface into space, you would pass through five major layers of the atmosphere, each with its own characteristics. Almost all weather occurs in the *troposphere*, the layer with the most oxygen. The ozone layer, which protects from excessive exposure to the sun's ultraviolet radiation, is part of the *stratosphere*. The stratosphere is also where commercial jets cruise to avoid turbulence. It is in the *mesosphere* that meteors burn up. Space shuttles orbited in the *thermosphere*, home of the International Space Station. Hubble and many weather and research satellites are in the *exosphere*.

This was the first flight of the Atmospheric Laboratory for Applications and Science payload, giving it the acronym ATLAS-1. Equipped with twelve highly specialized instruments from Belgium, France, Germany, Japan, the Netherlands, Switzerland, and the United States, ATLAS-1 carried out thirteen experiments. Among other things, these experiments were in atmospheric and solar science, as researchers were seeking more detailed information on matters such as the composition of Earth's atmosphere and the sun's output of energy. They were also seeking answers to a range of questions about the way the sun and Earth interact. (One instrument, the Imaging Spectrometric Observatory, was used to determine the makeup of the atmosphere down to trace amounts—that is, tiny, *tiny* amounts—of chemicals.)

ATLAS-1 also had a telescope that explored sources of ultraviolet radiation in the Milky Way and other galaxies.

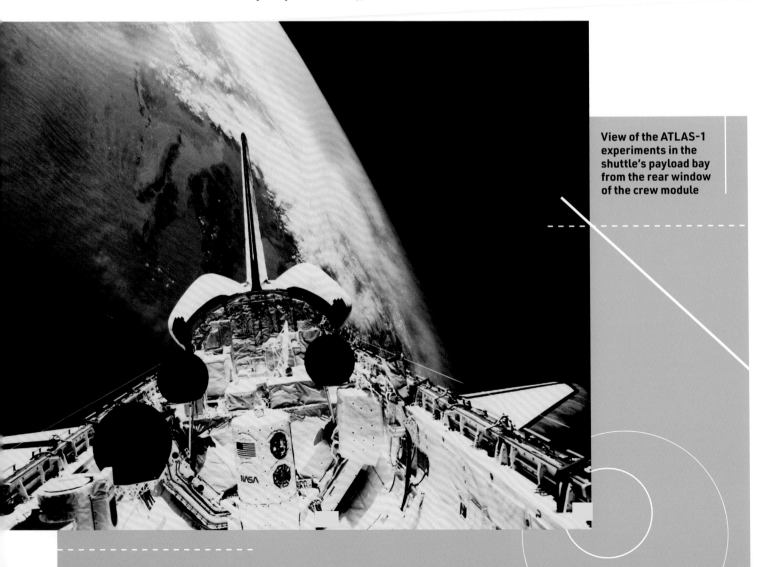

View of the ATLAS-1 experiments in the shuttle's payload bay from the rear window of the crew module

During our nearly nine-day mission, the crew worked around the clock: two teams, Red and Blue, in twelve-hour shifts. That way we could study the atmosphere in daylight and darkness all around the world, making the most of every minute of our 143-orbit flight.

The work consisted of monitoring ATLAS-1 and cueing up and overseeing its experiments.

On the Red Team were aeronautical engineer and naval flight officer Dave Leestma; British American astrophysicist Mike Foale; and aerospace, mechanical, and biomedical engineer Byron Lichtenberg.

On the Blue Team were Air Force pilot Brian Duffy; Belgian physicist Dirk Frimout; and a crewmate from the Hubble mission, Kathy Sullivan.

Dave and Brian were designated as shift commanders, authorized to maneuver the orbiter as needed to conduct our experiments.

As mission commander, I had overall responsibility for everything from preflight training to the conduct and safety of the vehicle and crew while on orbit. I could "play" on either team, and I served as backup on the ATLAS-1 experiments. My other work included assisting Brian and Dave in repositioning the orbiter from time to time so that instruments would be aimed at, say, the sun for this experiment or Earth for that experiment.

EARLY ON IN OUR PREFLIGHT TRAINING, I brought in a psychiatrist to meet with the crew and with our spouses to assist us in working up a psychological profile of each astronaut and their spouse. This would help us recognize and respond to any psychological stresses that might arise on orbit.

What made us tick?

What sorts of things got on our nerves?

Did we have any quirks?

I believed that the better we understood one another, the less likely it was that there'd be clashes or conflicts during the mission.

I like to think that bringing in that psychiatrist had a lot to do with the crew getting along extremely well, whether tending to ATLAS-1's experiments, carrying out our secondary experiments (such as the effect of weightlessness on vision), or simply relaxing.

Calling Long Distance

NASA has been relying more on psychological evaluations to prepare its crews for the challenges of long space flights. It's hard to communicate with family and friends on Earth when you're in space because there's a long delay—even simple voice or video transmissions take a while to arrive.

Kathy, Dirk, Brian, and me, eating together and enjoying a little downtime. See Brian's spoon floating above his tray?

During downtime, the crew had a lot of fun with the Shuttle Amateur Radio Experiment, or SAREX. Through SAREX, we chatted with everyday folks, including kids, who had access to ham radios. By the time we were ready to return to Earth, Kathy and Dave had talked with someone from each of our world's seven continents.

As during previous flights, one of my favorite things to do during downtime at night was to watch lightning around Earth as it went from cloud top to cloud top over hundreds of miles. It looked almost as if somebody were conducting an orchestra and light was flashing in response to the music.

Because we were the

Here I am making ham radio calls to fellow ham operators back on Earth through SAREX.

first shuttle mission to examine the mesosphere, we accomplished a significant number of scientific firsts. For example, using two of our ATLAS-1 instruments—the Space Experiments with Particle Accelerators (SEPAC) and the Atmospheric Emissions Photometric Imager (AEPI)—we were able to fire charged ions into the upper atmosphere and cause a small artificial aurora (or light show) in much the same way charged particles from the sun and other planets cause two large auroras at our north and south poles. SEPAC generated and fired the ions into the atmosphere. AEPI was a highly sensitive camera that detected and recorded the artificial aurora.

After our return to Earth, STS-45 had a post-flight bonus—a ten-day trip to Belgium, as guests of its king and queen! King Baudouin, as an amateur astronomer, was really, *really* interested in our mission. Dirk Frimout was Belgium's first astronaut, and after the mission, he was made a nobleman—a viscount!

At the king's request, the crew briefed the entire royal cabinet in his private briefing room in the Royal Palace of Brussels. This was to help the cabinet understand the importance of Belgium's continued participation in and financial support of the European Space Agency. As a result of Dirk's flight and his success, Belgium later flew a second astronaut, Frank De Winne, who became commander of the International Space Station in 2017.

Aurora australis, or the southern lights, photographed on April 2, 1992, the last day of our mission

Throughout the visit, we spent time talking with students in public schools and universities across Belgium. We shared photos and videos from our mission and helped the students understand the critical importance of taking care of our planet by trying to reduce all types of pollution and clean up our air, soil, and water.

In the Royal Palace of Brussels, Belgium. First row, left to right: My crewmate Dirk Frimout and his wife, Laurence; Queen Fabiola, King Baudouin, and Prince Philippe (who became king in 2013); and me and my wife, Jackie. In the second row are three of my crewmates and their spouses. Left to right: Patti and Dave Leestma, Jan and Brian Duffy, and Tamara and Byron Lichtenberg. (Crewmates Kathy Sullivan and Mike Foale weren't able to make the trip to Belgium.) Mission managers and key scientists involved with the mission are among the other fine folks in this photograph.

STS-60 mission patches in English and Russian

Peace

NEARLY TWO YEARS AFTER STS-45, on February 3, 1994, I was star sailing once again.

Once again aboard space shuttle *Discovery*.

Once again as mission commander.

And this mission, STS-60, was a most historic one.

It was the first time a Russian star sailor—called a cosmonaut—was a member of a space shuttle crew. This joint US-Russian mission was the first flight in the Shuttle-Mir Program. Mir was the Russian space station.

Given how historic it would be, was I super-excited when offered the opportunity to command this mission?

Not excited. No way!

I had zero desire to work with Russians!

Zero! Zero! Zero!

I grew up during the Cold War, when Russia was the most powerful republic in the Soviet Union—the United States' archenemy. During the Vietnam War, the United States backed South Vietnam, and the Soviet Union backed North Vietnam. As a Marine Corps pilot, I had essentially fought against Russians.

The Soviet Union dissolved in 1991, so that period of hostility between the two superpowers had ended only a few years before I was offered command of STS-60.

Work with a Russian in space?

No way!

At the time, I was NASA Assistant Deputy Administrator, and George Abbey, who was the special assistant to the NASA Administrator, urged me to at least meet the two cosmonauts in the running to serve as an STS-60 mission specialist. One was Sergei Krikalev, a mechanical engineer and champion

A Virtual Meeting

Sergei and I hadn't met yet in person, but we had met virtually. When I was commanding STS-45 and he was on Mir, we spoke using ham radio gear. At the time, Sergei was stuck. After the Soviet Union dissolved, it took the Russians a while to negotiate replacing Mir's crew. Sergei spent ten months in space instead of the originally scheduled five.

aerobatic airplane pilot. The other was Colonel Vladimir Titov, a MiG-21 fighter pilot.

I took George Abbey's advice. I met with Sergei and Vladimir twice: in DC, then in Houston, both times over dinner. We talked for hours about our families, our children, and our dreams for the future of the world. I was really impressed with Sergei and Vladimir—I found them to be terrific human beings. Good-natured. Thoughtful. Compassionate. My *No way!* became a thunderous

Yes!

In the end, Russia's space agency, Roscosmos, decided that Sergei would be the one to fly with us. By the end of our eight-day mission, Sergei and I were on our way to being friends for life.

We learned invaluable lessons from each other during the flight. We were able to adapt best practices of the Russian space program and those of NASA over the course of our training and the actual flight. A good example was finally adopting the Russian practice of allowing crews to make minor repairs as needed without waiting for approval or direction from mission control.

Now back to STS-60.

Like me, pilot Ken Reightler (aerospace and aeronautical engineer and former Navy test pilot) and mission specialists Sergei Krikalev, Jan Davis (aerospace and mechanical engineer), Ron Sega (physicist and electrical engineer), and Franklin Chang-Díaz (a crewmate on my first shuttle flight) were all thrilled about our primary objective: to deploy the Wake Shield Facility, the first satellite for producing semiconductor material in space.

It was a "facility" because it contained a heating element that took two materials, gallium and arsenic, and melted them for deposit in alternating ultrathin layers on small (about three inch by three inch) metal square "plates" to make gallium arsenide wafers. Back on Earth, each wafer would be cut up into teeny-tiny segments and used to make electronic components such as transistors for use in computers, radios, TVs, and other electronic equipment.

The theory was that in this special ultra-vacuum area, we'd be able to produce very pure semiconductor material that would conduct electricity much faster than semiconductor material made on Earth.

The term "Shield" in Wake Shield comes from the round shape of the satellite. Think of Captain America's vibranium shield, only much larger. The term "Wake" comes from the fact that by flying around Earth with its rim pointed toward the planet, the shield forces the very few molecules of air in space to fly around it like water around the bow of a ship, leaving an area behind the shield similar to the wake of water behind a sailing ship.

THE PLAN was for the unmanned flying saucer–like Wake Shield Facility to be lifted from the shuttle payload bay with an RMS, as had happened with the Hubble Space Telescope. Once released, the Wake Shield would free fly on its own for two days, then we'd fly the shuttle back to it and use the robotic arm to bring it into the payload bay again. Once we returned to Earth, the treasure trove of semiconductor wafers would be processed and made into ultra-fast computer chips.

It was a great plan, but . . .

We weren't able to release the Wake Shield from the robotic arm. The attitude control system, which is used to keep the satellite correctly oriented in space without any physical connection to *Discovery,* malfunctioned. It kept shutting down each time we attempted to start it. We didn't dare release the Wake Shield from the RMS for fear of this $12.5 million satellite going out of control and winding up lost in space.

In the end, we kept the Wake Shield on the RMS above the payload bay, activated the heater in the facility, and managed to make a few gallium arsenide wafers. Back on Earth, theory became fact: semiconductor material made in space did conduct electrical current much faster than wafers produced on Earth. So on a basic level, yes: mission accomplished. Still, we were deeply disappointed that we hadn't been able to deploy the Wake Shield Facility.

From Shuttle-Mir to the ISS

By the time the Shuttle-Mir Program ended, in June 1998, other Russian cosmonauts had flown aboard shuttles, and American astronauts had flown aboard the Russian Soyuz spacecraft. American astronauts had also lived on Mir, forerunner of the International Space Station (ISS). The ISS was begun in 1998, with the launching and combining of the Russian Zarya power and propulsion module and the US Unity connecting node.

An incredible bond and level of trust developed between the Russian and American teams. This was a direct result of the success of our STS-60 mission and the integration of Russian cosmonauts into our shuttle crews, crew trainers into all our training facilities, flight controllers into each other's mission control centers, and flight surgeons and other medical personnel into each other's clinics.

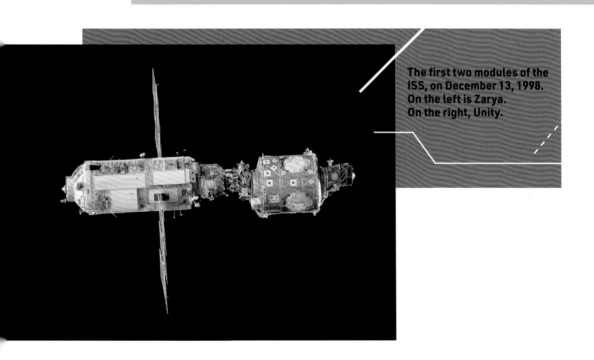

The first two modules of the ISS, on December 13, 1998. On the left is Zarya. On the right, Unity.

Learn a Little Russian!

Mir (pronounced myeer) is Russian for both "world" and "peace."

Soyuz (SOY-oos) means "union."

Zarya (ZAH-ryah) means "dawn" or "sunrise."

We later learned that the problem with the attitude control system could have been avoided had we done a more thorough test of the system before flight. To save money, the manufacturer of the Wake Shield Facility had eliminated a critical ground test that would have uncovered a problem that could have been fixed. This was a painful reminder of the importance of *thorough* preflight testing.

EVEN THOUGH all didn't go as planned, I have such fond memories of STS-60.

My best memories have nothing to do with preflight training or liftoff.

Nothing to do with any of the experiments we conducted.

Nothing to do with being an astronaut, really. (And certainly nothing to do with the Wake Shield Facility!)

My best memories have everything to do with my growth as a human being through my relationship with Sergei, with experiencing the wonderful fact that working toward common goals and missions can bring people from different cultures together.

Prejudices can fall away.

Borders and boundaries can fade away.

Long-lasting bonds can be forged to replace hatred.

That's what made STS-60, my fourth and final mission, so fantastic for me, Charlie B.

I'D KNOWN FOR SOME TIME that STS-60 would be my last flight. While being a star sailor was fun and exciting for me, for my family it was emotionally taxing, especially after the *Challenger* accident. Launch was the most difficult for my wife, Jackie, while the time on orbit was particularly hard on my kids. And landings were tough on everyone.

They didn't share this with me until after my third mission. Right after

I returned, I was assigned to NASA HQ in Washington, DC, to serve as Assistant Deputy Administrator. My family may have thought that this was a subtle signal from NASA leadership that my flying days were over, but when I shared that I was being considered to command STS-60, they made it clear to me that this would be it for my flying career. As much as they loved being part of the NASA family, they'd had all the "fun" they could take.

The decision to make STS-60 my final shuttle mission made each aspect of training and the flight emotionally charged for me because I knew it would be the last time I experienced those moments.

Hanging up my spacesuit was *hard*, but after I did, like my family, I was at peace.

Ken and me, rehearsing on the flight deck of the crew compartment trainer in the shuttle mock-up at JSC

After the *Challenger* accident, we developed a number of escape scenarios for crews in case something happened that wouldn't allow a safe landing in the shuttle. An escape pole was installed in the mid-deck of the shuttle that could be configured for the astronauts to attach a parachute line that would guide them out of the explosively deployed side hatch wearing parachutes. This is a photograph of Ken coming out the side hatch in our simulator facility. He would drop several feet to a safety pad to simulate a bailout.

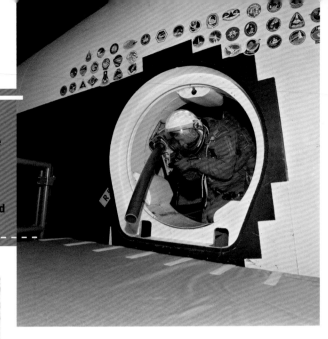

Vladimir Titov in bailout training in JSC's Weightless Environment Training Facility. When the two cosmonauts arrived in the States, Sergei was fluent in English and Vladimir spoke not one word of English, but he learned to speak it quite well during our year of training for the mission. (When I first met them, I spoke no Russian—and unfortunately, I still really don't.)

Following a launch meal and a briefing on the weather, here I am in the Suit Room at KSC, where I put on my launch and entry suit—in an emergency, this suit provides oxygen and pressurization to a crew member if cabin pressurization is lost. A suit technician is conducting a thorough checkout of the emergency oxygen system, the G-suit, and the communications system in the helmet and communications cap, which is worn under the helmet and contains earphones and a microphone.

A G-suit, or antigravity suit, is an inflatable undergarment that comes into play during reentry and landing—when Earth's gravity is once again a force on an astronaut and could pull blood too rapidly from their head to their lower body. The G-suit puts pressure on the lower body to stop blood rushing from the head and causing dizziness.

Crew walkout from KSC's Operations and Checkout Building. We are on our way to *Discovery* at Launch Pad 39A. Stepping lively behind me: Ken Reightler, Jan Davis, Sergei Krikalev, Ron Sega, and Franklin Chang-Díaz.

To guard against crew members contracting infectious diseases such as chicken pox, ten days before our scheduled launch, the crew was quarantined in a "health stabilization" facility at JSC. Seven days is believed to be the incubation period for most communicable diseases, so ten days in quarantine got a crew member through any possible infection. Three days before launch, we flew down to the KSC, where we moved into the Astronaut Crew Quarters to complete our preflight isolation period.

Launch time was 7:10:05 a.m. Eastern Standard Time on February 3, 1994

We're squeezing through the tunnel between *Discovery* and SPACEHAB-2 (short for Space Habitation Module-2), a pressurized workspace.

The variety of experiments conducted in SPACEHAB included ones related to improved pharmaceuticals and immune system disorders. To the right is the RMS used on this mission, Canadarm.

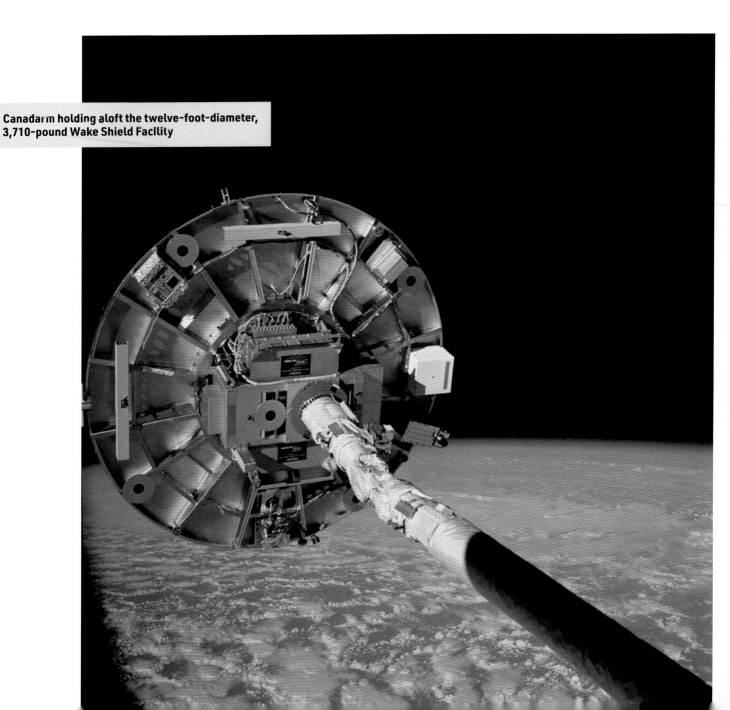

Canadarm holding aloft the twelve-foot-diameter, 3,710-pound Wake Shield Facility

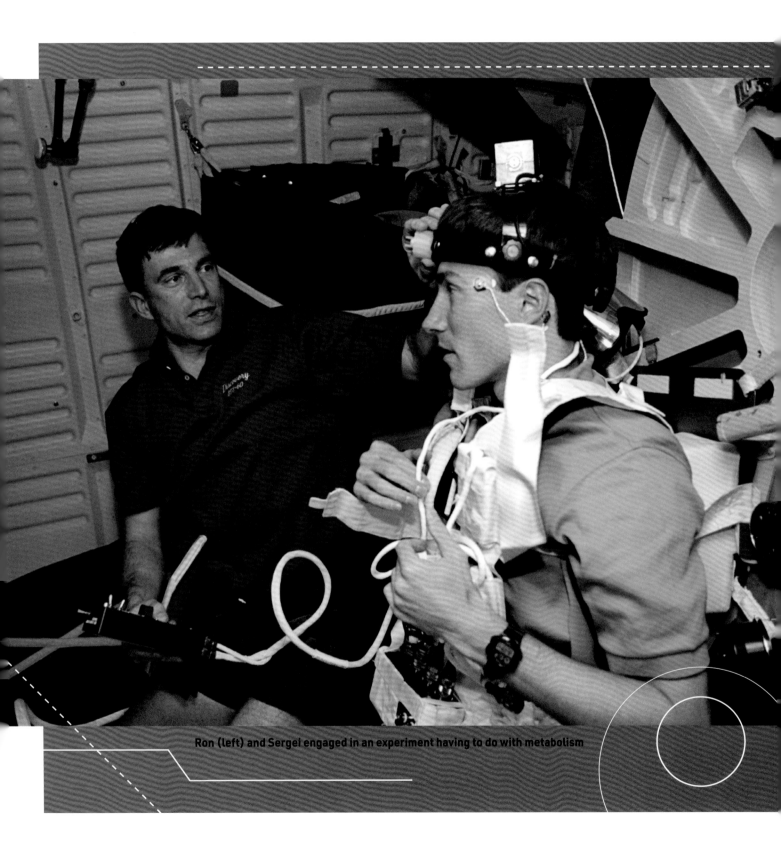

Ron (left) and Sergei engaged in an experiment having to do with metabolism

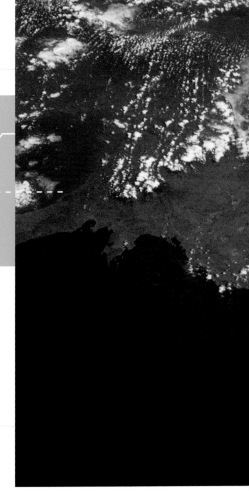

February 9, 1994: *Discovery* was up above Franklin's native Costa Rica, as well as Nicaragua and part of Panama. During our mission, Franklin conducted a video tour of the orbiter in Spanish for Costa Rican TV.

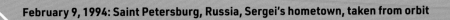

February 9, 1994: Saint Petersburg, Russia, Sergei's hometown, taken from orbit

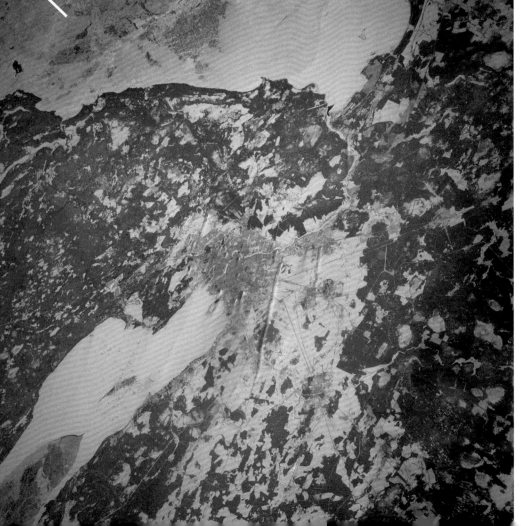

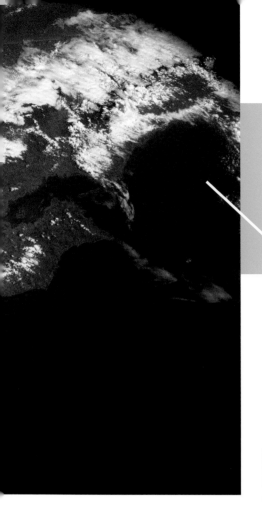

February 10, 1994: The Grand Canyon taken from orbit

Strapped into my Commander's seat aboard *Discovery*, right before executing our deorbit burn for our return to Earth and successful completion of STS-60

Our safe landing at KSC on February 11, 1994, at 2:19:22 p.m. Eastern Standard Time

Sergei and me on November 20, 2016, twenty-two years after we flew together. This photograph was taken at the Russian Mission Control Center in Korolev, Russia. It was my first time returning to Russia as NASA Administrator, and I was there to view the November 18 launch of NASA astronaut Peggy Whitson, cosmonaut Oleg Novitskiy, and European Space Agency astronaut Thomas Pesquet aboard a Soyuz spacecraft for their six-month mission on the ISS. Right before this photo was taken, Sergei and I were viewing mission data from the Soyuz crew vehicle as it approached the ISS.

The ISS was completed in 2011. This photograph was taken on March 7, 2011, by an STS-133 crew member aboard *Discovery*.

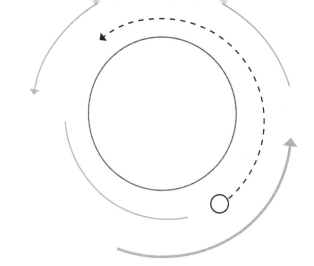

Author's Note

GROWING UP IN COLUMBIA, SOUTH CAROLINA, in the days of Jim Crow, I never thought about becoming an astronaut. But when I was a child, one of my favorite Saturday-morning activities—when Black people could only sit in the balcony of the local theater—was to go to see Flash Gordon sci-fi films, in which Flash routinely flew off to Mars in his spaceship.

In junior high school, I watched *Men of Annapolis*. This TV show, which premiered in 1957, was about life at the US Naval Academy in Annapolis, Maryland. I immediately fell in love with the Academy and decided that I wanted to attend college there. I knew nothing about the Navy or Marine Corps (which is part of the Department of the Navy), but that didn't matter. I wanted to wear that sharp white dress uniform with the high-necked collar and walk the historic "Yard," the name of the Academy's campus.

To attend, I needed to be appointed by a member of Congress or the vice president of the United States. I didn't have any luck writing my two US Senators and my Congressional Representative, all white, so my only real hope of getting into the Academy was an appointment from Vice President Lyndon B. Johnson.

12/3

1 encl

DEC 4 - 1963

2123 Barhamville Road
Columbia, South Carolina
November 28, 1963

The President of the United States
The White House
Washington, D.C.

Mr. President:

It was indeed an honor for me to hear from you last Spring, while you were serving as Vice President, in regards to my request for consideration for appointment to the entering class of '64 of the U.S. Naval Academy at Annapolis.

Then you requested that I write you after July 1, when you would know if you had any vacancies at the Academy.

I am still very interested in becoming a Midshipman and possibly making the Navy a career. Would you, therefore, refer me to someone who will be able to consider my application, since I am not eligible for a Presidential appointment.

I would appreciate very much your help in this matter.

Respectfully yours,

Charles F. Bolden Jr.

Charles F. Bolden Jr.

My letter to President Johnson

But on November 22, 1963, at the beginning of my senior year in high school, President John F. Kennedy was assassinated and Lyndon Johnson became president. I had been writing him since he had become the vice president in preparation for requesting an appointment from him, so any hope I had of getting into the Academy seemed to be over. My mom encouraged me not to be deterred, but to write to the president and remind him of our correspondence about an appointment to Annapolis. So I pulled out our old manual typewriter and typed a letter to the president pleading for help getting an appointment. I never heard back from him directly, but not long after I sent that letter, a Navy recruiter showed up at my door, asking if I was the young man wanting to go to the Naval Academy. Several weeks later, a retired federal judge from Washington, DC, visited—he'd been dispatched by President Johnson to travel around the country identifying qualified Black and Hispanic high school students interested in attending one of the nation's military academies. The next thing I knew, I received an appointment to the US Naval Academy from a Black congressman, William Levi Dawson of Chicago, Illinois.

MY FOUR YEARS as a midshipman at the Naval Academy (1964 to 1968) were filled with excitement, disappointment, struggles, even rare cases of discrimination, but in the end, I completed my studies, earned my bachelor's degree, and chose to accept a commission as a second lieutenant in the US Marine Corps.

I was a top performer throughout my training at the Basic School in Quantico, Virginia, where we were trained to become rifle platoon commanders and lead ground Marines. My Naval Academy class standing allowed me to pursue flight training. My wife, Jackie, and I moved a lot, first to Pensacola, Florida, where I began a year and a half of flight training, then to Meridian, Mississippi, for basic jet training, then back to Pensacola for carrier qualifications and aerial gunnery training, and finally to Kingsville,

Texas, for advanced jet training. That's where, in May 1970, I received my gold wings as a naval aviator.

I was the number-one graduate in my flight school class, so I got to select my aircraft. I chose to fly the A-6 Intruder with assignment to the Marine Corps Air Station in Cherry Point, North Carolina, for training and preparation to go to Vietnam to fly combat missions during the Vietnam conflict.

In my early Marine Corps career, I served in a variety of capacities, from squadron pilot to Marine Corps recruiter and officer selection officer (responsible for selecting officer candidates). Eventually I went to the US Naval Test Pilot School in Patuxent River, Maryland, where I was trained to become a naval test pilot. My job was to conduct test flights on various jets to certify them for use by the naval service. That's where I met the great Dr. Ron McNair, who embarrassed me into summoning up the guts to apply to NASA's astronaut program.

After I hung up my spacesuit in 1994, I returned to the operating forces of the Marine Corps until retiring in 2003. During those nine years, I enjoyed a whole other career as a general officer in the Marine Corps, living and serving in the United States, Kuwait, and Japan. I retired after serving as the commanding general of the Third Marine Aircraft Wing—the largest air wing in the Marine Corps—headquartered in San Diego, California.

Much to my surprise, several years after I retired from the Marine Corps, I was back at NASA! In 2009, President Barack Obama nominated me, Charlie B., to be NASA Administrator (equivalent to the chief executive officer, or CEO, in a civilian company).

In nearly eight years as Administrator, my accomplishments included the triumph of the *Curiosity* rover landing on Mars in 2012; the 2016 start of the Juno mission, which is helping us understand the planet Jupiter more completely; increasing the number of satellites observing Earth; and continuing progress toward the launch of JWST in December 2021.

NASA's X-59, a supersonic aircraft. It's so quiet that even when it's traveling faster than the speed of sound, there's no *BOOM-BOOM*! Developed during my time as Administrator, it rolled out in January 2024.

Not forgetting that the first *A* in NASA stands for Aeronautics, we also focused our attention on the agency's aeronautics programs and its goal of developing airplanes that can travel faster, farther, quieter—and greener.

On the left is the Hubble Space Telescope's iconic *Hubble Ultra Deep Field* photo, and on the right is one from JWST showing the identical portion of deep space using its greatly improved optics system. Notice the greatly improved resolution and richness of the image from JWST, whose power is estimated to be one hundred times greater than Hubble's.

Among my most challenging missions as Administrator was finally retiring the Space Shuttle program in 2011, after thirty incredible years of history-making operations. This also meant overseeing the transition from the space shuttle system to a new era of exploration, relying on civilian launch vehicles such as those from SpaceX, Northrop Grumman, and Boeing to carry our cargo and crews to the International Space Station.

Additionally, we developed the Space Launch System and the Orion crew capsule for eventually carrying astronauts back to the moon and on to Mars. Added to that, we created NASA's Space Technology Mission Directorate, responsible for developing the technology that will make future exploration missions successful.

A 2015 artist's concept of space probe Juno reaching Jupiter. Launched on August 5, 2011, Juno entered orbit around Jupiter on July 4, 2016.

THIS BOOK IS MY STORY of life as a NASA astronaut. I wrote it to tell my five grandchildren of the fourteen thrilling and rewarding years I spent training, supporting others preparing to fly to space, and flying my own four space shuttle missions, which changed my life forever. I want them to read about my exciting experiences and about the fun of spaceflight. I also want them to hear from me how my entire perspective on our great planet Earth was profoundly altered by seeing it in its beauty and grandeur from the vantage point of low Earth orbit—something fewer than six hundred people in human history have had the opportunity to see as of this writing.

Mikaley, Kyra, Talia, Walker, and Lenox were all born years after my final space shuttle mission in 1994, and I hope they will be able to travel on my flights with me through my words and the images in the pages of this book.

To them and others who read this book, I say follow your passion! Study hard, work hard, and never be afraid of failure.

A color-enhanced view of Jupiter based on three photographs Juno took on February 12, 2019

Time Line

My brother, Warren (center), with Mama, Daddy, and me (on the right) in the 1950s. I have no idea who the other child is.

AUGUST 19, 1946
Born in Columbia, South Carolina, to Ethel Evangeline Martin, a teacher and librarian, and Charles Frank Bolden Sr., a teacher and football coach (and a World War II veteran).

Playing with friends Pete Pendergrass (center) and Edith Hammond (left) in the 1940s

My brother, Warren (left), and me in 1959, with Mama at her motel in Atlanta, Georgia, after she received her master's degree in library science from Atlanta University. Daddy took the photo.

1946	1947	1948	1949	1950	1951	1952	1953	1954	1955	1956	1957	1958

SPRING 1958
Graduated from Carver Elementary School in Columbia, South Carolina.

The whole family in September 1964, during the Naval Academy's Parents' Weekend. We are standing in front of the commandant's house.

Daddy and me in September 1964, during the Naval Academy's Parents' Weekend at the end of Plebe Summer (freshman orientation)

Here I am in 1962, at the National Science Foundation Summer Institute in Chemistry at Manchester College in North Manchester, Indiana. This was my first trip on my own outside the segregated South.

JUNE 5, 1968
Graduated from the US Naval Academy with a bachelor's degree in electrical science. Of the 830 graduates in the Class of 1968, I was one of only four Black men. (The Academy didn't admit women until 1976.) After graduation, I was commissioned as a second lieutenant in the Marine Corps.

JUNE 8, 1968
Married fellow C. A. Johnson High graduate Alexis "Jackie" Walker at the US Naval Academy Chapel.

SPRING 1960
Graduated from W. A. Perry Junior High in Columbia, South Carolina.

JULY 1964
Entered the US Naval Academy with the Class of 1968. I was part of the brigade boxing team, the chapel choir, and the glee club, and I served as president of the Class of 1968 for our first two years.

1959 1960 1961 1962 1963 1964 1965 1966 1967 1968 1969 1970 ▶ ▶ ▶

SPRING 1964
Graduated with honors from C. A. Johnson High School. While there I played quarterback on the football team, played the timpani and percussion in the concert band, sang in the varsity choir, served on the staff of the school newspaper, served as student government president, and was a member of the National Honor Society.

JUNE 1967
Appeared with the Naval Academy glee club on *The Merv Griffin Show* in Philadelphia as part of Army-Navy football weekend.

MAY 12, 1970
Designated a naval aviator.

Mama, Daddy, and me in 1965, after Easter service at the Naval Academy Chapel. The tall cadet to my right is Paul Reason, who became the first Black four-star Navy admiral. The other cadet is Jimmy Frezzell, who left the Academy at the end of Plebe Year.

From the 1968 *Lucky Bag*, the US Naval Academy yearbook

CHARLES FRANK BOLDEN JR.

"Coming to Navy from Columbia, South Carolina, Charlie brought with him a never-ending supply of confidence and humor that earned him the respect and admiration of all who met him (and there were few who didn't). . . . Never too busy to help, [he] will be remembered for his ability to meet any situation with just the right amount of seriousness and levity necessary to make it right."

This photo was taken in 1986, after my first shuttle mission, STS-61C, aboard *Columbia*. I am being introduced to the South Carolina state legislature by Governor Richard Riley before receiving the Order of the Palmetto, the highest award South Carolina's governor can bestow upon a South Carolina native.

At the same ceremony, I am presenting South Carolina's governor, Richard Riley, with a montage from the mission.

JUNE 9, 1971
Birth of our son,
Anthony Ché Bolden.

MARCH 17, 1976
Birth of our daughter,
Kelly Michelle Bolden.

MAY 29, 1980
Became an astronaut
candidate.

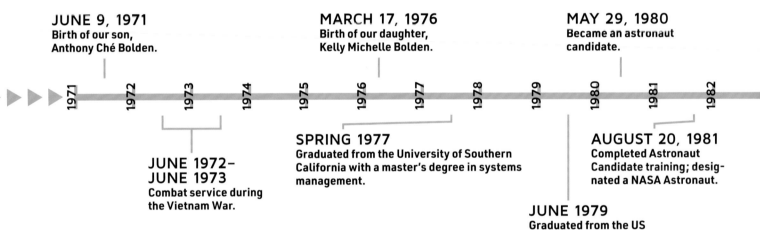

1971 1972 1973 1974 1975 1976 1977 1978 1979 1980 1981 1982

**JUNE 1972–
JUNE 1973**
Combat service during
the Vietnam War.

SPRING 1977
Graduated from the University of Southern
California with a master's degree in systems
management.

AUGUST 20, 1981
Completed Astronaut
Candidate training; desig-
nated a NASA Astronaut.

JUNE 1979
Graduated from the US
Naval Test Pilot School
at the Naval Air Station at
Patuxent River, Maryland.

I'm at KSC, about to rehearse some shuttle contingency landings in a T-38. This photograph was taken two days before our original launch date of April 10, 1990. (The launch was scrubbed because of a faulty valve in an auxiliary power unit.) "Panther" was my call sign, one I gave myself as a tribute to the Black Panthers and the work they did in Black communities during the height of the civil rights era.

Me with Reggie McNair in 1986, at one of the memorial services for his father, Dr. Ron McNair, and the other members of the *Challenger* crew

APRIL 1992–JANUARY 1993
Served as NASA Assistant Deputy Administrator. By then I had been given several technical assignments, including astronaut office safety officer, technical assistant to the director of Flight Crew Operations, special assistant to the director of JSC, chief of the Safety Division at JSC, and lead astronaut for vehicle test and checkout at the KSC. I had also received three NASA Exceptional Service Medals.

APRIL 24–29, 1990
Served as pilot of Space Shuttle *Discovery* on STS-31.

FEBRUARY 3–11, 1994
Served as mission commander of Space Shuttle *Discovery* on STS-60.

1984 1985 1986 1987 1988 1989 1990 1991 1992 1993 1994 1995 ▶ ▶ ▶ ▶

JANUARY 12–18, 1986
Served as pilot of Space Shuttle *Columbia* on STS-61C.

MARCH 24–APRIL 2, 1992
Served as mission commander of Space Shuttle *Atlantis* on STS-45.

JUNE 27, 1994
Returned to operating forces of the US Marine Corps.

Mama and me at the Naval Academy in June 1993, with my son—new Marine Corps second lieutenant A. Ché Bolden—after his graduation and commissioning

Here I am as nominee for Administrator of NASA, testifying at my Senate confirmation hearing before the Committee on Commerce, Science, and Transportation in July of 2009.

JULY 4, 1997
Promoted to major general and became the Marine Corps' highest-ranking Black officer (at the time).

MAY 6, 2006
Inducted into the United States Astronaut Hall of Fame.

1996 1997 1998 1999 2000 2001 2002 2003 2004 2005 2006 2007

SEPTEMBER 1, 2005
Incorporated JackandPanther LLC, a consulting firm on leadership, the military, and aerospace.

Me with some students from Albert Hill Middle School in January of 2011, during a visit to the MathScience Innovation Center to celebrate STEM

Entering the office on my first day as NASA Administrator—July 17, 2009

Welcoming President Barack Obama (on the left) to the NASA Space Conference at the Kennedy Space Center in April of 2010

SPRING 2017
Founded the Charles F. Bolden Group LLC, a veteran-owned small business specializing in space/aerospace exploration, national security, leadership, education (STEM+AD, meaning science, technology, engineering, and math plus art and design), and health initiatives. In May 2020, leadership of the company transitioned to my son, A. Ché Bolden, and my daughter, Dr. Kelly M. Bolden.

MAY 23, 2009
Nominated by President Barack Obama to be NASA's twelfth Administrator. (Confirmed by the US Senate on July 16, 2009.)

JULY 17, 2009
Began my duties as NASA's first Black Administrator.

APRIL 11, 2014
Received the Rotary National Award for Space Achievement.

JULY 2018–JUNE 2019
Served as US Department of State Science Envoy for Space.

2009 2010 2011 2012 2013 2014 2015 2016 2017 2018 2019 2020

AUGUST 27, 2012
Mine was the first recorded voice beamed to Earth from another planet. That planet was Mars. My message began, "Hello. This is Charlie Bolden, NASA Administrator, speaking to you via the broadcast capabilities of the *Curiosity* rover, which is now on the surface of Mars." I concluded: "This is an extraordinary achievement. Landing a rover on Mars is not easy—others have tried—only America has fully succeeded. The investment we are making . . . the knowledge we hope to gain from our observation and analysis of Gale Crater, will tell us much about the possibility of life on Mars as well as the past and future possibilities for our own planet. *Curiosity* will bring benefits to Earth, and inspire a new generation of scientists and explorers, as it prepares the way for a human mission in the not-too-distant future."

JANUARY 20, 2017
Retired as NASA Administrator.

OCTOBER 28, 2017
Inducted into the National Aviation Hall of Fame.

MARCH 26, 2019
Received the Smithsonian National Air and Space Museum's Michael Collins Trophy for Lifetime Achievement.

DECEMBER 17, 2020
Received the Wright Brothers Memorial Trophy.

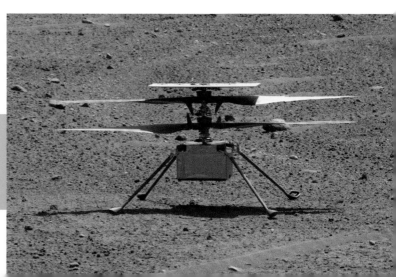

During my time as NASA Administrator, we developed much of the technology necessary for expeditions back to the moon and to Mars. Here is the helicopter *Ingenuity* on the surface of Mars—on April 19, 2021, it became the first aircraft to fly on another planet.

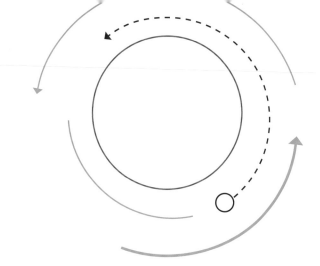

Source Notes

CHAPTER 1: DELIGHT AT DAWN

p. 4: "a delight at dawn": Chet Lunner, "Columbia: A Delight at Dawn," *Florida Today*, January 13, 1986, 1.

CHAPTER 2: THANK YOU, RON MCNAIR!

p. 9: On astronaut candidate applications in 1979: Howard Benedict, "Husband Joins Wife on US Astronaut Team," *Paducah Sun*, May 30, 1980, 10-A.

CHAPTER 3: TICK, TICK, TICK

p. 16: "If your last name . . . for a nickname": Robert L. "Hoot" Gibson, interviewed by Jennifer Ross-Nazzal, November 1, 2013, in Houston, Texas, NASA Johnson Space Center Oral History Project, Edited Oral History Transcript, https://historycollection.jsc.nasa.gov/JSCHistoryPortal/history/oral _histories/GibsonRL/GibsonRL_11-1-13.htm.

CHAPTER 4: FLOATING ABOVE MY SEAT

p. 32: "Welcome to space, rookie": Chet Lunner, "Columbia Gets Joyful Sendoff," *News-Press* (Fort Myers, Florida), January 13, 1986, 1.

CHAPTER 6: WHAT SOUND DOES A SPACE TURKEY MAKE?

p. 47: "It's hard to go somewhere . . . and study science": John Noble Wilford, "Shuttle Landing Is Planned Today," *New York Times*, April 29, 1990, 22.

p. 48: "Welcome back . . . next fifteen years": Lee Siegel, "Telescope Mission Rolls to a Stop," *York Daily Record* (York, Pennsylvania), April 30, 1990, 4A.

pp. 51–52: "What sound . . . Hubble, Hubble, Hubble": quoted in Casey Rentz, "The Supernova That Launched a Thousand Gorgeous Space Images," *Smithsonian*, July 17, 2018, https://www.smithsonianmag.com/science-nature /supernova-launched-thousand-gorgeous-space-images-180969611/.

p. 52: On Leno making Hubble a verb: Nola Taylor Tillman, "Hubble Telescope at 25: The Trials and Triumphs of a Space Icon," Space.com, April 20, 2015, https://www.space.com/29148-hubble-space-telescope-history-25-years.html.

CHAPTER 7: IGNORE-O-SPHERE

p. 55: "We are very honored . . . crew of *Atlantis*!" : AP, "Atlantis Astronauts Salute 'Star Wars' Creator, George Lucas," *Star-Tribune* (Casper, Wyoming), March 31, 1992, B7.

TIME LINE

p. 91: "Coming to Navy . . . make it right": *Lucky Bag* (Annapolis: US Naval Academy, 1968), 246.

p. 95: "Hello. This is Charlie Bolden . . . distant future": "First Recorded Voice from Mars," NASA Jet Propulsion Laboratory, August 27, 2012, https://www.jpl .nasa.gov/news/first-recorded-voice-from-mars.

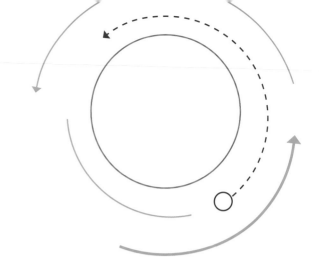

Image Credits

p. 13: Invision Frame/Shutterstock.com

p. 31: Courtesy of the *Los Angeles Times*

p. 32: Courtesy of Robert L. Gibson

p. 64: Courtesy of Viscount Dirk Frimout; Belgian Space Agency;
PS-2 STS-45 (ATLAS-1)

pp. 90–93 (except for the photo of Charlie B. wearing his Panther helmet):
Courtesy of the Ethel Evangeline Martin Bolden papers, South Caroliniana
Library, University of South Carolina, Columbia, SC

p. 95 (top): Joe Marino-Bill Cantrell/UPI/Alamy

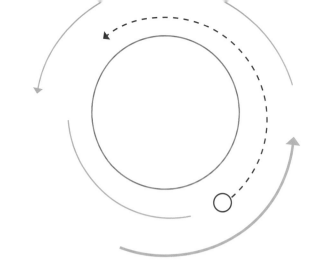

Index

Page numbers in italics indicate images or captions.

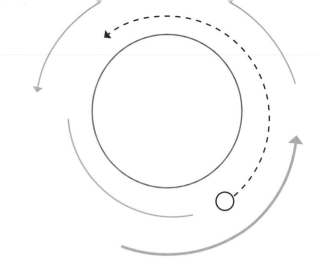

Acknowledgments

EVER GRATEFUL to Karen Lotz for her hearty embrace of this project and to Kharissia Pettus, who also championed the project early on.

And there's editor Olivia Swomley. Thank you so much, Olivia, for your enthusiasm, deft editing, and excellent questions.

Thanks is also due to others in the Candlewick family: copyeditors Betsy Uhrig and Jacqueline Houton; senior director of graphic production Gregg Hammerquist; designers Rachel Wood and Carolynn Decillo; and proofreaders Jason Emmanuel and Julia Gaviria.

For your generous assists on various matters, thank you former astronauts Bob Cabana, Mike Foale, Dirk Frimout, Brian Duffy, Hoot Gibson, Mike Lampton, Ron Sega, and Kathy Sullivan; McKenzie Lemhouse, assistant librarian, Medford Library, University South Carolina, Lancaster; Graham Duncan, head of collections and curator of manuscripts at South Caroliniana Library, University Libraries, University of South Carolina, Columbia, South Carolina; Todd Hoppock, interim head of user services at South Caroliniana Library, University Libraries, University of South Carolina, Columbia, South Carolina; Sheva Moore, NASA librarian and video researcher; Connie Moore, NASA photo researcher; Danny Van Hoecke, multimedia librarian and space teacher with the Euro Space Society; and Bert Ulrich, NASA multimedia liaison. I am also grateful to Bob Jacobs (deputy associate administrator of the NASA office of communications at the time of writing) and Bill Ingalls (NASA contract photographer) for their frequent assistance in locating and obtaining photos from the NASA archives. Much appreciation to Jason Neubert and Ralph Drew of the *Los Angeles Times* as well.

And I would be remiss if I did not also thank literary agent Jennifer Lyons for her feedback on drafts and overall support.

Perhaps more than any other person, I must acknowledge the partnership of Tonya Bolden! What are the chances of being paired with someone with the same last name who treats you like a blood relative? I owe her all the credit in the world for pulling me along on this project after I had struggled on my own for more than twenty years. Thank you, Tonya, for your guidance and counsel, your hand-holding, your advice, your patience, and most importantly, your wonderful writing.